Praise for Carla Hannaford's books

"**Smart Moves** by Carla Hannaford is a major work of profound importance to our understanding of child development and education. Through a brilliant analysis and synthesis of epochal research by neuroscientist Paul MacLean and the work of Paul Dennison in Educational Kinesiology, she opens a window of understanding into the workings of our mind/body that is not just dramatically pertinent to children, but to adults floundering in today's chaotic world as well.

"Rarely have I learned so much in so short and fascinating a time as in reading **Smart Moves**. Absorbing, formative and of serious value to all of us, it is hard to praise her work sufficiently."

— *Dr. Joseph Chilton Pearce, author of* **The Magical Child**

"It is seldom that we find something so really original and groundbreaking written about education. **Smart Moves** brings together in a remarkable synthesis knowledge from the neurosciences and information about how bodily movement, emotional expression, nutrition, and the social and physical environment influence learning. I have never seen a better guide to creating more effective learning situations in home and school."

— *Dr. Willis Harman, President, Institute of Noetic-Sciences*

"**Playing in the Unified Field** is a tremendously important book that all humans, from teens to adults would benefit greatly from reading, especially parents of all ages. Carla Hannaford has laid out a delightful set of articulate, authentic, and poetic images. I wish that I could have read this book before I became a parent!"

— *William A. Tiller, Professor Emeritus Stanford University, author of* **Science and Human Transformation**

T0159348

The Dominance Factor

How Knowing Your Dominant Eye, Ear, Brain, Hand & Foot

Can Improve Your Learning

Carla Hannaford, Ph.D.

SECOND EDITION
REVISED AND ENLARGED

GREAT RIVER BOOKS
SALT LAKE CITY

Book and cover design by M.M. Esterman

Copyright © 2011, 1997 by Carla Hannaford
Illustrations Copyright © 2011, 1997 by Great River Books

For further information contact:

Great River Books
161 M Street
Salt Lake City, Utah 84103
www.greatriverbooks.com

Library of Congress Cataloging-in-Publication Data
Hannaford, Carla
    The dominance factor : how knowing your dominant eye, ear, brain, hand, and foot can improve your learning / Carla Hannaford. — 2nd ed.
    p. cm.
    Includes bibliographical references and index.
    ISBN 978-0-915556-40-3 (trade pbk. : alk. paper)
    1. Cognitive styles. 2. Cerebral dominance. 3. Left and right (Psychology) 4. Mind and body. I. Title.
BF311.H3355   2011
153.1 — dc21   CIP

Printed in the United States of America   10 9 8 7 6 5 4

Contents

Illustrations

ACKNOWLEDGEMENTS

Colleen Gardner who first introduced me to a muscle checking way to determine Dominance Profiles.

Dr. Paul and Gail Dennison for for putting together the wonderfully usable Brain Gym and Vision Gym work from many modalities

Cherokee Shaner and Sandra Zachary, special education teachers in Hawaii who assisted me with the first research.

My mother Minnie who loved me in spite of my fully right blocked profile, and my daughter Breeze for her assistance, support, and insights that allowed for expression and usability of this work.

Esta Steenakamp and Rita Edwards, occupational therapists in South Africa who first validated the work within their practice.

Rosemary Sonderegger, Alfred Schatz, and all the other friends and educators worldwide for the encouragement to get my findings and format into print.

Judy Metcalf and Wanda McGee of the Washington, D.C. Area Edu-K Community who worked so many hours to help with the inital draft of the profiles. And to Margarita Hodge who provided encouragement and support to get the layout started.

Mark and Margaret Esterman whose skills and dedication have brought this work to fruition.

Helmut Meyer for his graphic inspiration.

Johanna Bangeman, Karen Kohler and all their fourth grade students who field tested earlier versions of the book in their classrooms.

Introduction

Because of the infinite variation in the way individuals are assembled, it must be assumed that the sentient properties of any one person, like his or her fingerprints could never be identical with those of another. It is probable, therefore, that there does not exist or ever will exist one person exactly like another. If uniqueness were an indispensable requirement for an evolving society, every person would be indispensable.

— Paul MacLean, *The Triune Brain in Evolution*

We all recognize the vast diversity of human beings — the diversity that makes each individual unique, interesting, bothersome, a delight, frustrating and a mystery to our own particular nature. Educators and psychologists have developed systems for identifying and generalizing diversity in order to better understand us. Such systems as the Meyers-Briggs Index, Bernice McCarthy's 4MAT system, Dunn and Dunn's Learning Styles assessment, Enneagrams and Howard Gardner's Multiple Intelligences are useful in general typing of human nature and learning styles. An understanding of learning styles is helpful for planning educational and training programs and for greater insight into individual behavior. My research and counseling work has been assisted by using a learning styles assessment system called Dominance Profiles.

This method of gauging and characterizing learning styles was first developed using muscle checking or applied kinesiology. The Dominance Profiles identify the lateral dominance of eyes, ears and hands in relation to the dominant brain hemisphere. These patterns of lateral dominance greatly influence the way that information is internally processed by an individual and consequently the kinds of learning activities he or she prefers.

My Experience with Dominance Profiles

I began using this method for determining dominance profiles in 1986 as a counselor for "alienated" intermediate school students. Introducing them to this new self-knowledge occasioned a great sigh of relief as they finally understood why they were experiencing difficulty both academically and personally. Their profiles 1) were simply not being accommodated by the current educational curriculum; 2) made it difficult for them to communicate when stressed; and 3) showed their difficulties were neither permanent nor pathological. As we (the students, their teachers and myself) explored their individual profiles, we worked together to create strategies for success.

When I first encountered the Dominance Profiles work, I found it particularly interesting. As a neurophysiologist who was also working with children, I liked the physiological basis of the profiles. This easily assessable, physically derived system allowed me to understand the organization of my students' brains, bodies and nervous systems. As both a scientist and a teacher, the linkage of learning styles to the learner's mind/body system made sense to me. Dominance Profiles assisted my students and their teachers to see their unique strengths and difficulties more objectively, more flexibly, and with deeper understanding. In my work with many learners and teachers, Dominance Profiles have continued to give me doorways to new and constructive insights into individuals rather than labels which confine and limit their view of themselves and their potential.

Having previously worked with the Meyers-Briggs Index, Dunn and Dunn's Learning Styles work and Bernice McCarthy's 4MAT system, I found the dominance profile work using muscle checking to be particularly interesting and accurate in accessing learning and behavioral styles. Lateral dominance patterns have far-reaching effects on our behavior, from how we interact in our relationships, to how we work, play and learn in new or stressful situations. Identification of learning preferences points to concrete ways to honor and aid each individual's methods of processing. Knowing about ourselves helps us to be more successful in all our relationships, our learning, our work and even our play.

In the process of presenting my findings, along with practical ways to use them, I have refined and clarified the distinctions among the Dominance Profiles. I've also done my best to confirm the neurophysiological bases of these variations, and to express those differences in words and images that are comprehensible to the layman as well as the professional. It has been important for me to simplify without distortion the methods for determining the profiles, and to provide strategies for benefiting from the information they yield. I have continued to incorporate the ever-expanding volume of neuroscientific and educational research, and have benefited greatly from the observations and contributions of many colleagues. This book is a compilation of the available research to date presented in an easy to use format. I believe that students, parents, teachers, counselors, business people, athletes, artists and couples will benefit greatly from this information.

Why Schools Need to Know about Dominance Profiles

The consequences of these findings extend beyond individuals. Over the years, among the many patterns I observed was one that revealed a discouraging incongruity between school teaching practices and the learning styles of a majority of students. In general, schools expect students to learn in a certain way, and students who do not fit this type are often viewed as inferior instead of merely as different learners. When I began to systematically observe students, I found a direct correlation between the labels the schools gave to the students, such as Gifted and Talented and Special Education, and their Dominance Profiles.

I feel the incongruous match between instructional methods and student learning profiles may be one of the many factors contributing to the increase in learning disabilities such as ADD, ADHD, Dyslexia and Emotional Handicaps in schools today. We have tended to label people without taking into consideration their normal, underlying profiles. This book then is not only written with the individual in mind, but also addresses school policy. In Chapter 6 I have included a formal study I undertook to objectify this tendency of the schools to mischaracterize certain learners. Hopefully this information will be useful for teachers and school administrators as well as parents and children who have been labeled in these often misleading and counterproductive ways.

Dominance Profiles became a valued addition to my own counseling work with Special Education and Emotionally Handicapped students. Used in Individualized Educational Programs (IEP's), the profiles informed and supported each child's understanding of his or her unique way of learning. (IEP's are usually year long educational goals, set up for each individual child and agreed upon by the teacher, counselor and parent of the child.) The Dominance Profiles also gave the parents and teachers an understanding of how to approach and honor each child's learning style.

How This Knowledge Changed A Life

The power of this knowledge is vividly illustrated in an experience I had when I first started using Dominance Profiles in my work as a counselor. It occurred at an IEP meeting I had arranged with a single parent father. His 10 year old son had been in Special Education for 3 years. During that time, the father had been called to the Vice Principal's office as often as twice a week to discuss his child's behavior — usually fights on the playground. So this father came to our meeting expecting the worst.

I had done a dominance assessment with his son which revealed him to have a Profile L. I explained that his son was the kind of learner who processed information with internal imagery, needing the whole picture and emotion to understand a concept, and who needed to move to anchor information. Profile L learners have great potential for creative and intuitive thinking, but they may have trouble communicating their thoughts and feelings when under stress. To reassure this worried father, I shared with him my suspicion that Albert Einstein was a Profile L learner. I surmised this because the great scientist didn't talk competently until age seven, and later in life often referred to his internal, image-laden inspirations that had sparked his groundbreaking insights. When I showed the profile to the father and explained to him that his son had more potential than he or other people knew, the man's face changed completely.

On the verge of tears, he told me things about his son he had never had an opportunity to tell the Vice Principal or anyone else. He told me how his son had gone through all the garbage cans after Christmas the year before, to find strings of discarded Christmas tree lights. He rewired all of them together and hooked the system up to his stereo system so that when a certain note sounded a particular light would flash. His son had also won a county marathon fun run for a local charity, coming in ahead of good runners much older than himself.

That father took home with him a deeper sense of his son as a whole person with great potential. As we worked with integrative activities during the school year, the fights decreased greatly and finally stopped by Christmas time. I was fortunate to run into this proud father and son a couple of years ago. The son is very successful, holding a place of great responsibility at work and going on for an advanced education.

Dominance Profiles are applicable and give us important information for understanding ourselves and others in educational situations, in our relationships (with partners, families, parents and children), in working situations and in creative endeavors.

By assessing the dominance of brain hemispheres, eyes, ears, hands and feet we arrive at 32 possible profiles — all of them perfect learning styles — and as Paul MacLean said, indispensable for an evolving society. Use these profiles as a way to understand that all people learn, act and react in their own specific way and at their own specific pace. Hopefully this will be a window to human diversity that allows us all to honor and be compassionate with our fellow humans.

May this work assist us to deeply understand the truth that each of us is an indispensable part of an evolving creative humanity.

✦ 1 ✦

What Is A Dominance Profile?

This book is about Dominance Profiles, a personal assessment technique that will help you determine your child's, spouse's, business partners, friend and your own learning style. With the information presented here, you will be able to discover the various stress and learning style preferences of yourself and those around you, and then follow up with useful strategies that assist learning, relationships, and creativity.

There are thirty-two different Dominance Profiles. You assign them by determining which of your eyes, ears, hands, feet and brain hemispheres are dominant (the ones used more frequently and more adeptly). People display all sorts of arrangements of dominance. You may, for instance, have a dominant left hand but a dominant right foot. You may have a dominant right eye but a dominant left ear. In my research I have found that a mixed dominance pattern is the most common.

I believe your lateral dominance is basically innate, developing at around 9 weeks in utero as the Moro Reflex for survival, develops. At that time, it appears that the developing embryo establishes "lead" functions (a lead hand, foot, eye, ear and brain) in order to react quickly in a survival situation. Since survival is our most primary need, these functions become hardwired in the brain and determine how we will respond during a life threatening or stressful situation to protect ourselves.

Using the ears as an example helps the understanding of how these lead functions work. The hearing mechanism begins developing very early in the embryo (as early as 23 days after conception) and is fully developed in the newborn baby. When laid on their back or stomach, the newborn will turn their dominant ear out as a sentinel to listen for danger. If danger is perceived, the baby will respond with the Moro Reflex[2] where the hands and feet fly open and the baby cries. This action has the potential to bring help and/or scare away an intruder. You will notice that when you are in a new situation, you will most likely sleep with your dominant ear out to alert you to any new sounds that might mean danger. But when you are in the safety of your own home, you will sleep with your dominant ear down to cut out the familiar sounds around you so you can sleep soundly.

Because these functions are established (hardwired in the system) so early, they become the familiar way we approach new learning, whether in the classroom, business setting or in human relationships. As you educate yourself and learn new skills and adaptive strategies for learning, you normally grow beyond the constraints of your basal profile. However, your basal profile will still influence your behavior throughout life — particularly when you are learning something new, being confronted with a new situation and when you are under stress. As research into embryonic and fetal development yields greater knowledge, we will better understand how basal dominance patterns become established.

Dominance Profiles

The thirty-two profiles supply information about how we take in, assimilate, and process sensory information and then respond to and express new learning and understanding. They are offered here as useful guides for students, parents, teachers, counselors and anyone else who chooses to support optimal learning and relationship skills.

The profiles provide important clues about a learner's preferences in school, at home and at work. They help us to understand and anticipate which people may have difficulty with particular tasks and types of information. They even suggest practical tips for the educational environment, such as who should be given hands-on learning opportunities, how to approach such visual learning tasks as reading, how to present new information to particular learners, or where they should be seated in a classroom. The profiles also give us valuable information for understanding ourselves and others: in our relationships with family, friends, business associates and in our creative and work endeavors, and strategies for success in all those arenas.

Why does dominance affect so many things about the way we learn and behave? To understand this question, you need to know about the nervous system links from the brain hemispheres to our eyes, ears, hands and feet.

Our Learning Preferences

If you were to ask someone to name the part of the body they learn with, they would most likely answer — the brain. And they would be partially correct. This answer only covers part of the picture because the brain, as marvelous as it is, cannot learn all by itself. It needs information. From our greater understanding of neurophysiology, we are realizing that the brain is basically a "meaning maker." All parts of our body supply the raw information that the brain uses to learn about the world. It takes information about our outer world from the sensory receptors throughout our body (at least nineteen sensory receptors according to Rivlin and Gravell), filters it according to what we believe is real, and then makes meaning of that information. The eyes, ears, hands and feet are part of that exquisitely adapted sensory system. Research is showing that all our higher cognitive processes are grounded in bodily experience, such that the brain's low-level sensory and motor circuits do not just feed into cognition: they are cognition. One cannot process the plot of a story without simulating the bodily sensations it evokes. The simple act of making a facial expression affects both how we feel and how we interpret emotional information from another person's face.[3, 4]

In addition, we're not all the same in the ways we use our bodies' learning organs. For instance, we all favor one hand over the other, one foot over the other, one eye over the other, even one ear over the other. When it comes to our brains, we tend to favor one brain hemisphere over the other also. This tendency to prefer one side to the other is called lateral dominance.

Some people learn better by seeing things, some prefer to hear about things, some to handle things. There are a whole host of learning preferences that people can exhibit. These tendencies are innate and they contribute to our unique learning styles. Particular learning styles are neither good nor bad. They are merely leanings toward certain types of perception and preferences for, and ease with, certain kinds of learning tasks.

This book attempts to determine and explain learning preferences in light of lateral dominance patterns. In large part, an individual's learning style depends on the particular ways that his or her learning organs are neurally linked.

When taking in new information, or — significantly — in times of stress, we have greater access to those senses that are directly linked to the dominant brain hemisphere. More specifically, under stress or with new learning, our sensory intake is facilitated when the dominant eye, ear, hand and foot are on the opposite side of the body from the dominant brain hemisphere.

Tasks that are facilitated by our particular neural wiring are more familiar for us and we tend to rely more on these familiar ways to learn. These crucial linkages will be explained more as we proceed. Let's begin with the brain.

The Brain's Two Hemispheres

Our brains are composed of two distinct hemispheres which are connected in the middle by a bundle of nerve fibers called the corpus callosum. Each hemisphere develops and processes information in a specific way. To put it in simple terms, the **logic hemisphere** (usually on the left side) deals with details, the parts and processes of language and linear analysis. By contrast, the **gestalt** — meaning whole-processing or global as compared to linear — hemisphere (usually the right side) deals with images, rhythm, emotion and intuition. Roger Sperry and Michael S. Gazzaniga did some of the first conclusive

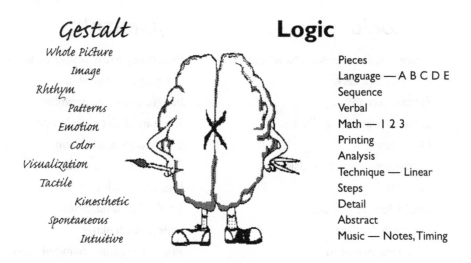

Gestalt

Whole Picture
Image
Rhthym
Patterns
Emotion
Color
Visualization
Tactile
Kinesthetic
Spontaneous
Intuitive

Logic

Pieces
Language — A B C D E
Sequence
Verbal
Math — 1 2 3
Printing
Analysis
Technique — Linear
Steps
Detail
Abstract
Music — Notes, Timing

Figure 1: The Brain's Two Hemispheres

research in the 1960's regarding the differences in the two hemispheres. That research has continually been upgraded as we acquire more sophisticated research tools.[5] But generally, Figures 1 and 2 give an overview of the main processing differences between the two hemispheres.

Many people are aware of this hemispheric differentiation and are familiar with the terms left-brained and right-brained. So why use different terms? Because an extremely small percentage (much less than 1%) of people are **transposed**, and process the logical functions on the right and gestalt functions on the left. To distinguish them by function, I use the terms logic and gestalt instead of left and right.

The corpus callosum between the hemispheres acts as a superhighway allowing quick access to both linear detail in the logic hemisphere and the overall image in the gestalt hemisphere. When there is good communication between the two halves, the result is integrated thought. The more that both hemispheres are activated by use, the

Logic

Processes from pieces to whole

Parts of language

Syntax, semantics

Letters, printing, spelling

Numbers

Techniques (sports, music, art)

Analysis, logic

Looks for differences

Controls feelings

Language oriented

Planned, structured

Sequential thinking

Future oriented

Time conscious

Structure oriented

When Under Stress

Tries harder, lots of effort

Without results

Without comprehension

Without joy

Without understanding

May appear mechanical, tense, insensitive

Gestalt

Processes from whole to pieces

Language comprehension

Image, emotion, meaning

Rhythm, dialect, application

Estimation, application

Flow and movement

Intuition, estimation

Looks for similarities

Free with feelings

Prefers drawing, manipulation

Spontaneous, fluid

Simultaneous thinking

Now oriented

Less time sense

People oriented

When Under Stress

Loses the ability to reason well

Acts without thinking

Feels overwhelmed

Has trouble expressing

Cannot remember details

May appear emotional or spaced-out

Figure 2: Differences between the Two Brain Hemispheres.

more connections form across the corpus callosum. The more connections, the faster the processing between both hemispheres and the more intelligently and creatively we are able to function. Actually, it is necessary to use both hemispheres of the brain to be maximally proficient at anything. But, as noted above, we all have a degree of hemispheric dominance and in times of stress, or new learning, people will exhibit a preference for either logic or gestalt processing.

Gestalt Dominant Processing

The Gestalt side of the brain is the first to develop. Between pre-birth and about age seven the "surf is up" for this hemisphere as it takes in the global aspects of the environment, analyzing spatial relationships, and becoming the primary seat of emotional arousal, as it specializes in detecting and responding to unexpected and behaviorally relevant environmental stimuli. Because our first need is survival, the gestalt hemisphere becomes the primary controller in potentially dangerous situations.

This hemisphere's main function is processing novel situations, all the curiosity, spontaneity and new learning that occur in babies and young children, and on throughout our lives as we encounter new challenges. It works from the bottom up, beginning with development of the survival reflexes and intuition, then elaboration of the sensory/motor systems that expand our global awareness of the world and each other. Thus, this hemisphere is organized to rapidly and creatively respond to a novel challenge. Brainstorming is akin to what occurs within our gestalt hemispheres sensory/frontal lobe processing system. In Brainstorming, we are charged with a novel challenge and must determine its dynamics and come up with a creative solution.

Memories in the gestalt hemisphere are organized and recalled as overall contextual patterns. This has been called the relational brain because face recognition and the ability to interpret emotional facial expressions occur here. Regarding language, even though it is non-verbal, this hemisphere provides the images, emotions, rhythm and dialect of language that guide comprehension and the ability to extract a theme or the main point from a story, series of events, metaphors, concepts and abstract ideas.[6] Gestalt preferential learners welcome rich sensory/motor experiences throughout their lives.

The gestalt dominant learner (Profiles I – PP) has not been as positively reinforced in our educational system, making up the vast majority of children in our Special Education programs (note Figure 24, p. 149). "All learning begins with gestalt hemisphere exploration, something often ignored in schools that give students answers to questions they didn't ask. They thus learn the answer, but don't really understand the question (or challenge)." [7]

Often the Gestalt brain has been referred to as the creative brain, but in reality, creativity demands whole brain functioning. The table in Figure 2 is a simplified summary of the basic differences between the two brain hemispheres.

Logic Dominant Processing

Normally the "surf is up" for the Logic hemisphere of the brain around age eight through age sixteen to twenty-one when quick integrated processing between both hemispheres becomes more common in a survival-free environment. The Logic hemisphere appears to be specialized in processing familiar challenges and well-established patterns of behavior, under ordinary and familiar circumstances. It translates the successful initial responses of the Gestalt hemisphere to a challenge, into a more linear, established routine that is activated whenever a like challenge occurs. In this way, it exhibits self-motivated behaviors that come from the top down as we mirror our family and cultural behaviors and set up linear, personal routines that allow us to exist within our specific cultural challenges.

Although both hemispheres are active in processing most cognitive functions, the relative level of involvement shifts from right to left over time with increased familiarity and competence.

The Logic hemisphere deals with grammatical language (alphabet, words, syntax, spelling) as an efficient, established procedure to enhance communication between humans. Wernekes and Broca's areas of the brain exist in the Logic hemisphere and initiate verbal language. People with a stroke in the logic hemisphere will be unable to talk.

The Logic hemisphere controls the remarkable dexterity of the right hand, now believed to be the fairly recent link from manual tool making to speech and language.[8] This hemisphere also deals with numbers in a linear way, arithmetic calculations, planning and favors step-by-step mastery of technique in learning any new skill. The preferential logic dominant learner (Profiles A – HH) tends to be more positively reinforced in our present language/math oriented educational system and are more often labeled gifted and talented (note Figure 24, p. 149).

Cross-lateral Control

In addition to these hemispheric specialization differences, there is another difference between the two sides of the brain. They each control a different side of the body. The brain has a crossover pattern, such that each side of the body communicates with the opposite brain hemisphere. Almost all sensory-motor functions on the right side of the body are either realized or controlled in the left hemisphere. And all sensory-motor functions on the left side of the body are realized and controlled in the right hemisphere. Hence, the right ear communicates with the left hemisphere, and the left ear with the right hemisphere. The left hand sends information to and is controlled by the right hemisphere, and the right hand sends and receives signals from the left hemisphere, and so on throughout the whole body.

Given the tendency toward hemispheric dominance, it is not surprising that we prefer those sensory-motor functions that are facilitated by our particular patterns of lateral dominance. Those senses and motor functions (physical movements) where the dominant eye, ear, hand or foot is on the opposite side of the body from the dominant hemisphere communicate more effectively with the brain even in times of stress.

For example, if your dominant brain hemisphere is on the left side and your dominant eye is on the right side, then you are able to take in visual information at any time, even in a stressful situation. Vision will be a preferential way of learning for persons with a

dominant eye opposite their dominant hemisphere, and therefore they will be considered visual learners.

It is during times of new learning or stress that the non-dominant brain tends to radically decrease its functioning, leaving the dominant brain to carry on primary functioning. This state of decreased function in one hemisphere is called a unilateral state. By contrast, when both hemispheres are functioning together optimally, that is called an integrated state and is the key to higher level reasoning and creativity.

Impact of One-Sided Processing

During stress only the dominant senses, hand and foot opposite the dominant hemisphere will be adept at processing. Furthermore, we are limited in our access to those senses and physical movement functions that are dominant on the same side of the body as the dominant brain hemisphere. This is called a receptive or expressive **limited** profile.

Profile L (see page 100) for instance, is fully limited in the unilateral state because all the learning components — eye, ear, hand, foot and brain hemisphere — are dominant on the right side. During stress this person is unable to access most auditory and visual information and has difficulty moving gracefully and communicating. This kind of learner becomes overwhelmed by the whole picture, unable to see the details, and must have quiet time alone to process information internally. Because they have difficulty verbalizing, seeing or hearing under stress, they often get labeled "learning disabled" and end up in Special Education programs which can lead to more stress, which perpetuates their unilateral state.

By contrast, Profile A (see page 56) shows full sensory motor access in the unilateral state. Here, the left hemisphere controls the right hand and foot and gets sensory information from the right eye and ear. Even under stress, a person with this profile can access detailed, linear information visually and auditorially and can communicate details through language. This kind of learner usually does well on verbal and mathematical skills tests. However, such learners (since their gestalt — usually right — hemisphere is inhibited during stress) may experience difficulty understanding in emotional, imaginative ways. They may have trouble seeing the big picture ('not seeing the forest for the trees'), thus decreasing their comprehension of the information. They may also have difficulty accessing empathy and compassion which are key relationship skills.

We need both hemispheres working equally together for optimal learning. Even though the logic hemisphere is considered the language brain, we need the comprehension functions of the gestalt hemisphere to gain full language function. The same is true of creativity. Though the gestalt hemisphere has been considered the creative brain, it takes proper technique (logic hemisphere functioning) in art, music, dance, theater and sports to be highly creative.

Eye Dominance

From Figure 3 you can see that in an integrated state, we are able to take primary vision in through both eyes which includes both left and right eye fields. The view within the eye fields is then interpreted in the brain to give us our actual perception and analysis. Only 4% of vision actually comes through the eyes as primary vision, the other 96% is manufactured in our brains according to all our other senses and our "take" on reality.

Visually able learners have their dominant eye opposite their dominant brain hemisphere and they can access visual information even under stress. They will be helped by visual presentations of new or challenging information, such as charts, diagrams, pictures,

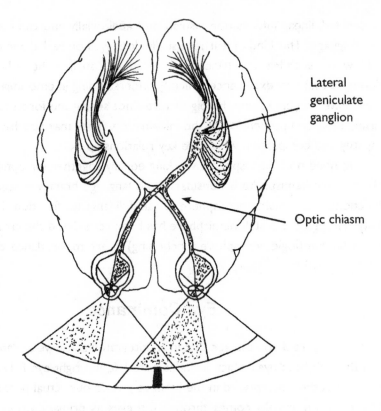

Lateral geniculate ganglion

Optic chiasm

Figure 3: Vision in an Integrated State

tables, posters, etc. Under stress, eye dominance will determine how visual information is primarily processed, depending upon which hemisphere the dominant eye communicates with.[9] Figure 4 illustrates the difference in vision for gestalt dominant and logic dominant learners. Logic dominant individuals whose opposite eye is dominant will only process the details in their visual field, missing the big picture. Gestalt dominant individuals whose opposite eye is dominant will look for the whole picture and miss the details.

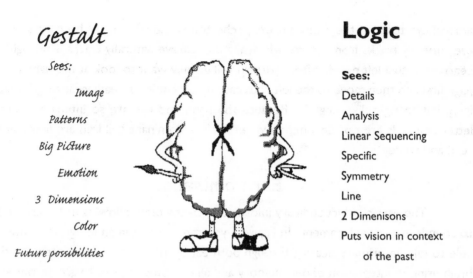

Gestalt	Logic
Sees:	**Sees:**
Image	Details
Patterns	Analysis
Big Picture	Linear Sequencing
Emotion	Specific
3 Dimensions	Symmetry
Color	Line
Future possibilities	2 Dimenisons
	Puts vision in context
	of the past

Figure 4: Differences in Vision for Gestalt Dominant and Logic Dominant Learners

In the **visual limited** profile, with the dominant eye on the same side as the dominant brain hemisphere, visual access is decreased during stress. Approximately half of all people, according to my research, are unilateral for eyes, (dominant eye on same side as dominant hemisphere). When a visually limited person, say a spouse, child or business partner is stressed, they may need to look away or close their eyes in order to take in what their partner, or a parent is attempting to communicate. This accommodation may cause a teacher, spouse, partner or parent to assume they aren't listening or paying attention. In actuality, they are doing their best to use what senses are not limited.

As you might imagine, eye dominance has important implications for reading. In normal eye teaming the dominant eye orchestrates the tracking of both eyes. The right eye naturally tracks from left to right while the left eye naturally tracks from right to left. Learners with a left eye dominant pattern will initially want to look at the right side of the page first and then move to the left, thus causing difficulties in reading languages that move from left to right, like English. Because the hand and eye are so intimately connected, letter reversals are not uncommon when left eye dominant children are first learning to read and write.

Ear Dominance

The ears conduct auditory information to the brain, allowing us to hear and listen to sounds in our environment. In Figure 5 you can see that in an integrated state, we are able to take in primary hearing through both ears. The sound is then interpreted in the brain using an integration of our memory and all our other senses to give us our auditory perception and analysis of the world.

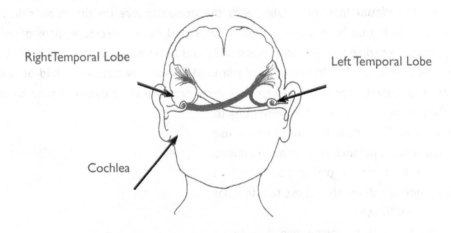

RightTemporal Lobe

Left Temporal Lobe

Cochlea

Figure 5: Hearing in an Integrated State

Auditory able learners have their dominant ear opposite their dominant brain and prefer an auditory presentation when learning new or challenging information. There is a distinct asymmetry in the nerve networks leading from each ear to the brain hemispheres as seen in Figure 5. Note that the darkened nerve fibers coming from the right ear to the left hemisphere are thicker than the darkened nerve fibers from the left ear  to that hemisphere. Because of this asymmetry, the right ear primarily sends information to the left hemisphere while the left ear primarily sends information to the right hemisphere. Therefore, gestalt dominant individuals with the opposite ear dominant will preferentially listen for the tone, metaphor, story, dialect and emotion of the information.

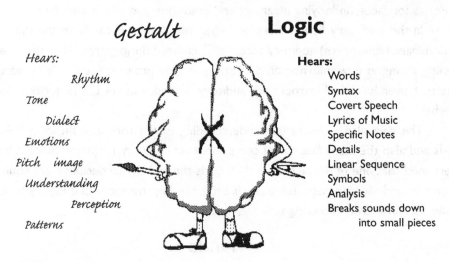

Gestalt

Hears:

Rhythm

Tone

Dialect

Emotions

Pitch   image

Understanding

Perception

Patterns

Logic

Hears:

Words
Syntax
Covert Speech
Lyrics of Music
Specific Notes
Details
Linear Sequence
Symbols
Analysis
Breaks sounds down
into small pieces

Figure 6: Differences in Hearing for Gestalt Dominant and Logic Dominant Learners

Logic dominant individuals with their opposite ear dominant will preferentially listen for the details and linear progression of information. Figure 6 illustrates the differences in hearing for gestalt dominant and logic dominant auditory able learners.

The area of the brain that interprets sound information, the temporal lobe, has strong neural links to the area that processes memory and emotion in the limbic system.

Learners with an auditory preference often have good memories — dependent on their hemispheric link. Logic hemisphere dominant individuals whose opposite ear is dominant have good memories for numbers, formulas, spelling, names, and other detailed information. Gestalt hemisphere dominant individuals whose opposite ear is dominant tend to have good memories for faces, underlying meanings and emotions, and whole concepts.

In the **auditory limited** profile (when the dominant ear is on the same side as the dominant hemisphere) auditory access is decreased during stress. For these learners, listening, taking in new information by hearing it, may prove difficult. My research indicates that over half of all learners are auditory limited, and yet the majority of teaching is verbal.

The ears also facilitate our understanding of the tone and meaning behind the words and also the many fast sound components in ordinary language. Since it has been determined that one of the factors of dyslexia is the inability to decipher fast sound components in ordinary language, (sh, th, s, ch, etc.), the improvement of auditory functioning should be considered in dealing with dyslexia.

Hands

A large area of the sensory and motor cortexes of both hemispheres of the brain, are dedicated to the hands. The hand feeds information to the brain through touch and

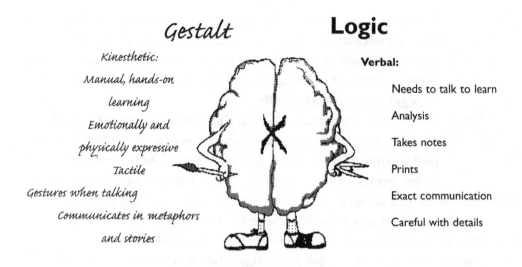

Gestalt

Kinesthetic:

Manual, hands-on learning

Emotionally and physically expressive

Tactile

Gestures when talking

Communicates in metaphors and stories

Logic

Verbal:

Needs to talk to learn

Analysis

Takes notes

Prints

Exact communication

Careful with details

Figure 7: Differences for Gestalt and Logic Access to the Dominant Hand

movement. Hands are also a means of expressing learned knowledge through gesture and writing. Interestingly, PET Scans of the brain show that when a person is speaking, there is increased activity in the areas of the brain associated with hand movements (motor and sensory cortexes of the neo-cortex). In fact, the hands are extensively involved in human communication, both in verbal and in kinesthetic (bodily) expression. Our patterns of dominance for brain hemispheres and hands distinctly influence how we prefer to express ourselves. Figure 7 illustrates the differences for gestalt and logic hemisphere access to the dominant hand.

Opposite handed logic hemisphere dominant persons (usually left hemisphere/right hand dominant) are **verbal learner able**. They tend to be verbally expressive in order to anchor information, learn and understand a relational situation.

They like to talk about what they are learning, and what's on their mind. They will talk even under stress. These learners can benefit from discussion or writing in order to anchor new information in memory.[10] But under stress they may be less able to express themselves with hand and body gestures (**kinesthetic limited**).

Logic hemisphere dominant persons with dominant hands on the same side (usually left hemisphere/left hand dominant) will be **communication limited** in the unilateral state. Under stress they have limited access to the kinesthetic, gestalt hemisphere and also will be limited in their verbal expression because of the homolateral brain/hand pattern.

It is interesting that approximately one tenth of the population is left-handed. Right handedness appears to be directly correlated with the development from gesture to verbal language. Left handedness appears to be more correlated with physical expressiveness (gesturing) and is more prevelant among artists, composers and the generally acknowledged great political thinkers, such as Albert Einstein, Greta Garbo, Matt Groening and Spike Lee.[11] Perhaps they are very integrated, or have had to become highly creative in order to get by in our right-handed culture that has designed scissors, can openers, circular saws, guitars, golf clubs and computer mice to fit that orientation. Many naturally left-handed children have been forced to switch to the right hand which some psychologists say can cause confusion in the brain, with the right hemisphere relegated to a subservient role and the left hemisphere becoming overburdened. Some studies show this can cause speech, reading and writing disorders.[12]

Gestalt hemisphere dominant persons tend to be kinesthetically expressive. They communicate well with their bodily gestures, and like to engage in physical action as they learn. Their gestures and body language can be very expressive. When the dominant hand is opposite the dominant gestalt hemisphere (usually right hemisphere/left hand dominant), the learner is **kinesthetically able**. Even under stress they can fully communicate kinesthetically. They are very manually kinesthetic, needing to have something in their hands or doing something with their hands in order to learn. They are emotionally and physically expressive and learn kinesthetically by manipulating objects, doing hands-on learning, and expressing their emotions with their whole body. Under stress, they will usually gesture in place of speaking (**verbally limited)**.

Gestalt dominant learners with their dominant hand on the same side (usually right hemisphere/right hand dominant) are **communication limited** under stress because of limited access to the verbal, logic hemisphere. Under extreme stress, they may instinctively strike out with their dominant hand when they can't find the words to express themselves.

With regards to the hand and learning, movement and verbal communication are essential to anchoring new information and should be integrated and frequently used in an effective curriculum.

Feet

A large area of the sensory and motor cortex is also dedicated to the feet. The feet provide a lot of information about the environment and balance. Current research is suggesting that going barefoot greatly assists children and the elderly in maintaining balance, and learning about their environment. The feet are controlled by the opposite hemisphere, which coordinates and commands movement of the feet according to muscular intention and hemispheric processing as shown in Figure 8. A person with a dominant foot opposite the dominant brain hemisphere is **movement able**. When the dominant

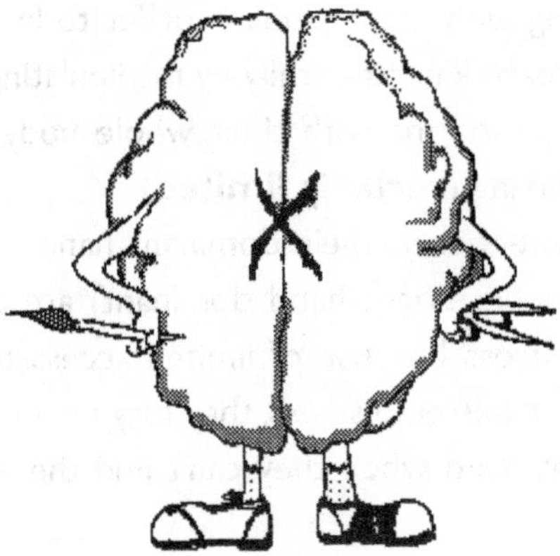

Gestalt

Logic

Moves:

Free form movement

Moves with emotion

Rhthymic

Spontaneous

Moves:

Planned movements

Follows step-by-step

instruction

Able to follow

specific dance steps

Figure 8: Differences for Gestalt and Logic Access to the Dominant Foot

foot is opposite the logic hemisphere, the person will feel comfortable making planned movements. These people are good at following step-by-step instructions in sports, dance and other movement activities, but may lack spontaneity in their movements.

If the dominant foot is opposite the gestalt hemisphere, the movements will be more spontaneous, free-form and guided by the rhythm. However, these people may have difficulty following step-by-step instructions.

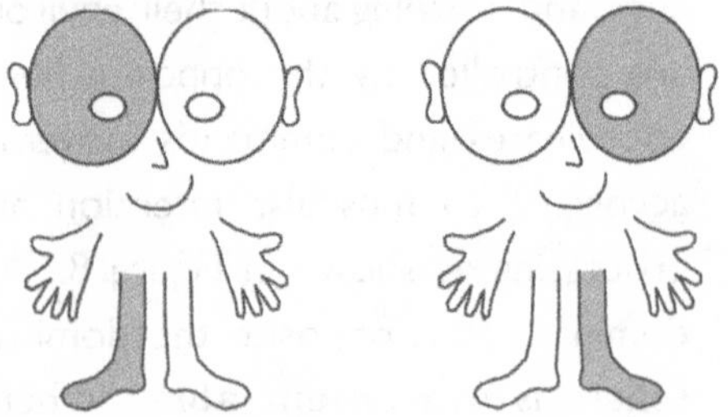

When the dominant foot is **movement limited** (on the same side as the dominant hemisphere) the individual will have difficulty moving forward under stress. Persons with limited feet will find that they initially tend to "stop in their tracks" unable to take immediate physical action

Access in a Unilateral State

Dominant Sense	Dominant Hemisphere	Learning Characteristic	Learning Preference
Right eye	Left	Visually Able	Logic/details
Left eye	Right	Visually Able	Gestalt/global
Right Ear	Left	Auditory Able	Logic/details
Left Ear	Right	Auditory Able	Gestalt/global
Right hand	Left	Verbally Able - Kinesthetically Limited	Logic/details
Left hand	Right	Kinesthetically Able - Verbally Limited	Gestalt/global

Limited in a Unilateral State

Dominant Sense	Dominant Hemisphere	Learning Characteristic
Right eye	Right	Visually limited
Left eye	Left	Visually limited
Right ear	Right	Auditory limited
Left ear	Left	Auditory limited
Right hand	Right	Communication limited
Left hand	Left	Communication limited

Figure 9: Learning Characteristics in a Unilateral State

when confronted with stressful circumstances. They may feel paralyzed and hold back until they understand the situation. If they do move, they may experience clumsiness resulting in bruises, skinned knees, or worse.

In contrast, persons with their dominant hemisphere opposite their dominant foot will continue to move under stress, maybe feeling like they are "running around like a chicken with its head cut off." They tend to plow on through, but their actions may be wasted because only half their brain is functioning.

The Dominance Profiles give information about the function of our eyes, ears, brain hemispheres, hands and feet when we are stressed or confronted with new learning. People can be limited in some senses and enabled in others. They may be visually and auditory able but hand and foot limited, or some other combination. Some have full access to all the senses and others are fully limited in their access during stress. In the next chapter you will learn some assessment techniques and have an opportunity to determine the Dominance Profiles of yourself and the other people in your life.

Whole-Brain Integration

"Wisdom emerges in older people who have developed a large repertoire of useful solutions to life's challenges [via the Gestalt Hemisphere], — and can effectively incorporate them into the resolution of new challenges [via the Logic Hemisphere]."[13]

The optimal learning and relationship state is one of whole-brain integration. In this state, both hemispheres are equally active all the time, thus accessing **all** sensory information and effectively communicating, moving and acting on the information. In an educational setting, the learning environment can be designed or improved to encourage whole-brain learning. For one thing, the setting should be stimulating but as stress-free as possible. As mentioned previously, stress increases unilateral functioning. Additionally, learners should be offered a broad spectrum of multisensory opportunities. If they can see visual presentations, hear auditory explanations, explain to someone else what they have learned, and get tactile opportunities to touch and take apart models, manipulatives, etc., there's a greater chance of matching all students' learning preferences. Another important ingredient of successful learning is the opportunity to move frequently — both to wake up the brain and to anchor learning.

A wide range of activities can be highly effective in integrating whole brain functioning and anchoring new learning for optimal success. Among them are Brain Gym®, Eurhythmia, Tai Chi, Qi Gong, singing alone or in groups, self-created music and dance sessions, cooperative (non-competitive) physical education programs, self and group-expressive art activities, drama and play acting, cooperative group solution finding and quiet reflective time. In Chapter Four, I will discuss many techniques and strategies to help you function in more integrated, whole-brained ways.

✳ 2 ✤

How to Determine Dominance Profiles

In this chapter you will learn how to assess Dominance Profiles. You can use these assessment techniques to determine the dominant eye, ear, brain hemisphere, hand and foot of any person. There are a number of ways to determine lateral dominance of the eyes, ears, hands, feet and brain hemispheres. Following are two methods that you may use for assessing yourself and others. The first is the self-assessment method, which is quick and usually reliable for assessing your **current** lateral preferences. For adults this may not necessarily be the basal profile. The self-assessment involves answering questions and noting observations about one's own behavior. If you are a teacher, a friend, a parent, or a spouse or co-worker, you can assist others in answering these questions about themselves. Often the less the subject knows about the assessment, the more accurate the results. So, if you want to know your own profile, it might be better to have someone read the self-assessment method below and assist you in performing the simple tasks described.

I have found it particularly easy to assess basal Dominance Profiles with children because they tend not to have preconceived notions of their dominance patterns nor have they as yet developed stable compensating strategies. Children come to this work with a sense of discovery and enjoy learning about their Dominance Profiles with their classmates, parents and teachers. When testing children you are fairly certain to arrive at their true basal profiles.

Adults however, may have some difficulty determining their basal Dominance Profiles because they have developed such stable compensating strategies. When I use the term basal Dominance Profile, I am referring to a pattern that is set up at about 9 weeks in utero with the advent of the Moro Reflex. However, the most accurate basal Dominance Profiles are obtained through muscle checking. Muscle checking is a technique used by kinesiologists and health professionals to help them understand people through the body's neuromuscular responses.

At the particular time of testing a number of factors may influence the outcome of the assessment. The subject may be very integrated at the time, using both brain hemispheres and both sides of the body fairly equally. Or, they may be favoring one side over the other because of the tasks they are currently engaged in — regardless of their basal profile. This **adaptive processing** will be discussed in greater detail in the next chapter.

Both assessment methods will be offered here. I suggest you start with the self-assessment method as it will give you valuable information about how you learn and respond at this moment in time. The muscle checking method, which is explained at length, though superior in accuracy especially for your basal profile, is more complicated to learn and will take more practice than the self-assessment method.

Introducing DomiKnow

Figure 10 is a character I've created to help you visualize and keep track of your assessment results. A darkened area of the DomiKnow indicates dominance in that hemisphere, hand, eye, ear or foot. The view of this character on the next page is the same view you would have facing another person. This will help you with your assessment of other people. When thinking about your own profile, remember, you will have to visualize yourself in the same orientation as the DomiKnow.

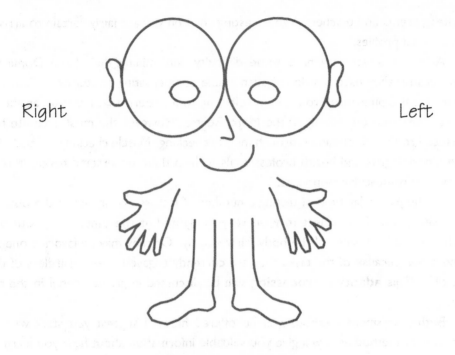

Right   Left

Figure 10: DomiKnow

As you go through the assessment, keep track of the results by darkening dominant areas in a blank DomiKnow. A set of blank DomiKnows are reproduced on page 189 at the end of this book.

The **Key to the 32 Dominance Profiles** on page 55 will help you find the profiles you are looking for. Please bear in mind that all profiles are perfect — but different — learning styles. No judgments about the superiority of some to others need be made. When viewed all together, the thirty-two profiles support a world that needs diverse abilities and multiple points of view. Also, please do not label learners. Dominance Profiles do not present the full complexity of any person nor do they indicate the infinite adaptive strategies that people develop to expand their capacities as they grow and learn.

I now invite you to obtain a blank DomiKnow from the back of the book and to assess yourself using the following method:

The Self-Assessment Method

Hand — Whichever hand you currently write with. You can assist other people in determining their dominant hand by offering them a pen or pencil at their body's midpoint (at waist level in the middle part of their torso). Whichever hand they reach out with to take the pen or pencil will be their current dominant hand.

Figure 11: Reaching Out at the Body's Midpoint

Eye — Hold your thumb out at arm's length, lining it up with a vertical structure (door or window frame, picture edge, etc.), focusing on it with both eyes. You are likely to see a double image — that is normal. Without moving either your thumb or head, close one eye, then open it and close the other eye. Whichever eye holds the image of the vertical object lined up with your thumb is the dominant eye.

Or, make a window by overlapping the two hands so there is a small opening between the thumb and forefinger of both hands. Hold the window at arm's length. With both eyes focusing through the window, line up an object (another person's face, a door knob, etc.). Without moving either your window or head, close one eye, then open it and close the other eye. Whichever eye holds the image is the dominant eye.

Figure 12: Making A Window with Hands for Determining Eye Dominance

Ear — Pretend there are people on the other side of a

wall across the room who are talking about you. Walk to the wall and put your ear close so you can listen to what they are saying. Which ear did you put against the wall?

Or, lay on the floor on your stomach and note which ear you put up to hear the sounds above you.

Or, hand the person being assessed a sea shell or empty cup at their body's mid-point (at waist level in the middle part of their torso). Ask them to listen to the sound of the shell or cup and note which ear they put the cup or shell to in order to hear the sound.

Foot — Step up onto a step or chair and notice which foot you used first. Or kick a ball and note which foot you kicked with. (It's useful to have someone observe you when you're not thinking about it).

Or, you might also lean far forward with feet together until you fall forward and notice which foot you step out on to catch yourself.

Or, to get a more accurate reading, have someone push you off balance from behind when you don't expect it. (Obviously, be careful with this last suggestion).

Brain Hemisphere — Use the Logic and Gestalt chart on page 20 to decide which hemisphere you currently access the most. This should give you some indication of your current brain dominance. However, the best test is to recognize how you would initially respond during a highly stressful situation. During stress, you rely more on your dominant brain hemisphere.

If you are **logic dominant**: when under stress your first response is to analyze the situation, write or talk about it and look for the specific reasons behind it. Your focus will be on the details, with a strong need to understand each aspect of the situation.

If you are **gestalt dominant**: when under stress your first response is to see the whole situation and feel the emotion. But you may be unable to decipher the details. You will have difficulty in breaking the whole situation down into the pieces of language to express it. Talking is not an initial response. Often you feel a strong need to physically move or express emotions.

Find your matching DomiKnow among the possible 32 Dominance Profiles. The **Key to the 32 Dominance Profiles** on page 55 will assist you to quickly find your profile.

The Muscle Checking Assessment

Muscle checking is a technique used to gain information from the body — about itself. Through muscle checking you can ask your body a question and it will give you an answer. The body, which of course includes the brain, knows itself — sometimes in ways that don't even enter into consciousness. At least 90% of what occurs in our bodies is subconscious. Every muscle and every organ in the human body is in communication with nerves. All the nerves, from the ones in your little toe to the ones in your big brain, are in communication with one another; making you a very complex information exchange system. By eliciting a response from muscles you can tap bodily information directly, especially things you might not consciously know.

To experience this, here is an experiment you can do with a friend or family member.

1.) While standing, think of something you really enjoy and have the other person use medium pressure to push on your upper back, right shoulder, left shoulder and the upper part of your chest. Notice how your muscles easily hold your body stable and erect against the pressure.

2.) Now think of something that is stressful in your life and have the person again use medium pressure to push on your upper back, right shoulder, left shoulder and upper front chest. Notice how the muscles do not hold you as stable against the

Figure 13: A Gentle Test for Stability

pressure. We even refer to this as "being thrown off balance" by the situation. These subtle differences in muscular response allow us to use muscle checking as an external indicator of internal (mental, emotional, physical) processes.

There is an art to muscle checking as there is with any worthwhile tool. It must be practiced to become proficient and skillful with it. Dr. David Walther's book on Applied Kinesiology or John Diamond's on Behavioral Kinesiology give an in-depth explanation of the art of muscle checking. My own explanation about why muscle checking works can be found in Appendix A on page 165.

Here, a very simple way of muscle checking will be introduced. This method requires two people, a facilitator and a subject. The facilitator will put questions to the test subject, who will answer through muscle responses. You could use any muscle in the body, but for ease we will use the deltoid muscle in the shoulder as the indicator muscle, a sort of truth detector, helping to obtain as accurate a Dominance Profile as possible.

To become familiar with the deltoid muscle:

1.) Stand with your right arm straight down and then touch your right shoulder with your left hand. Follow the muscle you feel at the shoulder down to the middle of the upper arm where the muscle comes to a point or delta. That is the deltoid muscle.

2.) Now, with the elbow straight, bring the arm up at a 90° angle to the body and "lock" the muscle so that it easily holds the arm up. Feel the deltoid muscle again. Notice that it has contracted to pull the arm up and is now easier to distin-

Figure 14: Locating the Deltoid Muscle

guish. Raise and lower the arm a few times so you really get a feel for the deltoid muscle.

We are looking for two specific states of the muscle, the "lock" and the "release." When the muscle is "locked" it feels similar to what you experienced when the muscles of the body held you stable while someone pushed you as you were thinking of something you enjoyed. The "release" feels more like the less stable hold you felt when someone pushed you while you were thinking of something stressful. During muscle checking, the examiner and subject will be checking for a clear "lock" or "release" of the deltoid muscle, in response to a question or stimulus.

Figure 15: "Locking" the Muscle at a 90⁰ Angle

To get a feeling for the amount of pressure the facilitator should apply to the subject's arm experience it on yourself.

1.) While standing, place two fingers of your left hand on the upper side of your right forearm between the wrist and the elbow.

2.) Bring the right arm up to a 45° angle, keeping the elbow straight, and lock the deltoid muscle.

3.) Notice how much pressure you have to apply with the two fingers of the left hand just to meet the pressure of the locked arm. It is usually a very light pressure of approximately 2 pounds if measured by a dynamometer. When muscle checking, the pressure does not have to be any greater than 2 pounds to obtain accuracy. To experience what we mean by a "release" let the right arm give under the 2 pounds of pressure from the left hand.

Figure 16: Applying Light Pressure for Self-Assessment

When you have had some practice with muscle checking you will be able to distinguish these two states, even when the differences are subtle and when the subject may not be aware of them. Again, this is an art as well as a "technique," and with practice becomes more and more accurate. Professional kinesiologists use this and similar techniques for many purposes, but this simple method should give you a basic tool to determine Dominance Profiles.

Figure 17: Preparing for Muscle Checking

Procedure For Muscle Checking A Subject

1.) Facing the subject, the facilitator invites the subject to lift their arm to a 45° angle and lock their deltoid muscle (Figure 17). The facilitator puts two fingers on the subject's arm a couple of inches above the wrist, and the other on the subject's opposite shoulder (right hand on left shoulder, or left hand on right shoulder, Figure 18).

Note: *This forms a stable tripod between the subject and the facilitator, also making it easier for the facilitator to apply less pressure, and to sense if the subject is recruiting other muscles. Recruiting other muscles to resist the pressure tends to distort the subject's true response.*

2.) The subject is instructed to breathe out (exhale) in an audible sustained way to indicate they are ready for the facilitator to check them.

Note: *By muscle checking during a sustained, audible exhalation, the subject is inhibited from recruiting accessory muscles to hold up the arm.*

Figure 18: Forming a Stable Position for Muscle Checking

3.) The facilitator then applies a *light*, even, downward pressure to the subject's forearm (during the exhalation) until both subject and facilitator feel the lock in the deltoid (usually 2 seconds). **Make sure you both feel a solidly locking deltoid before proceeding.**

Note: The muscle check is not a test of strength, but rather an accurate indicator check that leads to self-discovery. The subject should just lock the muscle easily without recruiting other muscles to try to be strong. That will invalidate the check.

4.) To feel how the muscle works as an indicator, muscle check having the subject say their name ("my name is_____"), and then muscle check with the subject saying a fictitious name ("my name is Pinocchio"). The muscle should easily lock when they say their own name and release with the fictitious name. Because we have said our names many times in our lives, saying our name is hardwired in the nervous system. Therefore, for most of us, we can easily say our name while doing a complex activity like driving a car, reading street signs, and holding our arm up. But when we say a fictitious name, the brain is busy looking for a connection to a foreign message, and the electrical connection to hold the arm up is decreased. You could also have the subject think of something they like and muscle check. The arm will normally stay up. Then have them think of a stressful situation and the arm will normally go down, because what makes a situation stressful is that we don't understand it and the brain is working on it, thus the message to the arm is decreased.

If the subject feels that the examiner is applying more pressure for one question than for another, that is an indication that the muscle has released and that other muscles are attempting to hold up the arm. Sensitivity to the lock and release, on the part of the subject will greatly enhance the accuracy of the muscle checking.

Note: If the subject is unable to get a good muscle lock (if the arm feels mushy), drinking water should help. When we are dehydrated, we don't have sufficient electrolytes to maintain optimal electrical activity between the nerves and muscle and therefore we may have trouble holding the arm up.

5.) Intention is essential in setting the muscle as a gauge. Both subject and facilitator must now set their intention to obtain an accurate **basal** Dominance Profile, otherwise a current (adaptive) or integrated profile may be obtained. Though these also give information about current processing, they don't tell our base preferential or unilateral pattern during new learning or stress.

The subject might set his or her intention to be at 9 weeks in utero, or think back to their earliest memory in order to access their most basal Dominance Profile. *Be sure to have subjects keep their eyes open during the muscle check, otherwise they tend to lose attention.*

Figure 19: Muscle Checking for Dominant Ear

6.) It is always best to get permission from the subject when doing any kind of muscle checking. Therefore, ask the subject verbally and then **with a muscle check**: "Are you willing to check for a basal Dominance Profile at this time?" If the arm locks, it is appropriate to continue. If the muscle releases, it is not appropriate to proceed.

If there is not a clear go-ahead by the body for the basal profile, ask if it is willing to check for a current profile. If the arm still indicates a NO response, respect that message and don't proceed.

Note: *The correct attitude of the facilitator and subject is to accurately get a muscle indicator response without concern for the outcome of the procedure. The subject and facilitator should have a sense of self-discovery — and let go all preconceived notions they might have about the subject's Dominance Profile.*

7.) To determine which hand is dominant, the facilitator asks the subject to bring attention first to one arm and then to the other while muscle checking each arm to find which arm locks and which releases. (Figure 18.) The dominant hand is determined by which side most clearly locks. Record the dominant hand on a blank DomiKnow.

Use the dominant arm as the indicator for all the rest of the checks.

8.) To determine the dominant ear, have the subject hold one ear lobe and bring attention to that ear while muscle checking the dominant arm (Figure 19). Do the same with the other ear. The dominant ear is the one being held when the indicator muscle most clearly locks. Record the dominant ear on the DomiKnow.

9.) To determine the dominant eye, have the subject touch the outside corner of one eye while looking at something, and muscle check the dominant arm (Figure 20). Do the same with the other eye. The dominant eye is the one being touched when the indicator muscle most clearly locks. Record the dominant eye on the DomiKnow.

Figure 20: Muscle Checking for Dominant Eye

10.) To determine the dominant foot, have the subject touch the upper part of one leg and bring attention to it while muscle checking the dominant arm (Figure 21), and then do the same with the other leg. The dominant leg is the one being touched when the indicator muscle most clearly locks. Record the dominant foot on the DomiKnow.

11.) To determine the dominant hemisphere of the brain, have the subject bring attention to and touch one side of their head above the ear while muscle checking the dominant

Figure 21: Muscle Checking for Dominant Foot

Figure 22: Muscle Checking for Dominant Brain Hemisphere

arm, and then the same with the other side of the head (Figure 22). The dominant hemisphere is the one being touched when the indicator muscle most clearly locks. Record the dominant hemisphere on the DomiKnow.

12.) Sometimes (extremely rarely), the hemispheres of the brain are transposed, which means the gestalt function is in the left hemisphere and the logic function is in the right. To establish where the logic function resides, have the subject count from 1 to 5 out loud and check the right arm. Then have them count out loud again and check the left arm. Counting only comes from the logic hemisphere. If the right arm locks, the numbers from the counting are coming from the left hemisphere, and that is considered their logic hemisphere. (Write 1,2,3 in the left hemisphere of DomiKnow.) If the left arm locks while counting, the numbers are coming from the right hemisphere, and that is their logic hemisphere. (Write 1,2,3, in the right hemisphere of DomiKnow.) In this latter case, the person is transposed and needs to read the section on transposition on page 53.

13.) Check the Key on page 55 and find the subject's matching DomiKnow from among the 32 possible Dominance Profiles.

⇥ 3 ⇤

The 32 Dominance Profiles

The profiles listed here are basal profiles. They describe the patterns of lateral dominance that we are born with. The learning behaviors associated with each basal profile describe reactions and tendencies of the learner in a unilateral state (when relying primarily on the dominant brain hemisphere). Therefore, our basal Dominance Profile gives important information as to how we most easily take in and process new learning, especially when it is challenging. It is the road map of our specific base learning style. When confronted with a new learning situation, we will access information most easily through our dominant senses (eyes or ears), and express (either verbally, with gestures or in writing) with our dominant hand. These basal patterns are most evident when we are learning something new and also when we are in a stressful situation.

The basal profiles described in this book are useful in clarifying potential learning blockages and suggesting possible integrative activities that help to establish more whole-brained learning.

But a word of **caution** is in order here. These profiles should never be used to label and type learners. They indicate ways that individuals are prone to respond, but not necessarily how they will always behave. It is dangerous to label people because it inhibits our ability to see their whole dynamic potential as unique individuals.

Adaptive Processing

Our brains are highly plastic/adaptable, able to change our dominant functions in the moment to be more effective in different situations, but under stress, we will return to the hardwired basal profile developed in utero. In relaxed situations we are not so bound by our basal Dominance Profiles, and are able to expand our capacities beyond them. We allow ourselves to develop learning strategies that work for us, which become our **adaptive processing** styles. In the past, for instance, many people learned to write with their right hands even though they were naturally left-handed. This is not a practice I advocate, but it does illustrate our great ability to adapt. People can train themselves to become good listeners, better at observing and deciphering visual information, more verbal, more physically coordinated, etc.

Another way we adapt is by becoming more cross-lateral in the ways we work and think. As we grow and learn we become much better at using both brain hemispheres together. This integration facilitates ease of sensory assimilation, processing and appropriate response.

Brain plasticity continues throughout our lives as the neural circuits, especially those specialized for learning, continue to adapt in response to experience.[14, 15, 16] Even in stoke patients, the neural circuits of the healthy hemisphere will take over the control of both sides of the body.[17] And interestingly, even people with hemispherectomies, where either the right or left hemisphere has been taken out or never developed, the other hemisphere will take over the needed functions for both.[18]

As a consultant working with large groups, I must be able to see, hear and speak, even under stress. My basal Dominance Profile is L, fully limited with no sensory access during stress, which means my first response is to totally shut down under stress. Presenting in front of large groups can be stressful for me. So over time I have developed adaptive strategies that I can access when under stress so I don't shut down when I am on the spot and need to be effective. The integrative strategy that seems to help me the most is movement. If you are ever in one of my courses, you will probably notice that I move a lot.

Many mature adults are highly integrated with good adaptive strategies and they may find it more difficult to relate to their unilateral, basal Dominance Profile. The basal Dominance Profiles still give valuable information as to how they will react and learn under the most severely stressful situations, and what will be are preferential learning styles with new learning.

No Labeling Please

It is important to remember that there should be no judgments about people because of their learning profiles. Everyone has the capacity to learn, but we tend to learn in our own unique ways. The last thing we need in education is more misleading and limiting labels. Knowing the elegant flexibility and adaptability of human beings, the basal profiles give a starting point for understanding. I think of these profiles simply as models that help us to honor each learner, so we can create an optimal learning environment that supports each learner's ability to access and work from their integrated whole-brain state. The following profile descriptions are rather simplified explanations that only touch on the high degree of complexity the profiles in this book represent.

Transposed Brain Hemispheres

As noted previously, a small percentage of the population is transposed, meaning the logic hemisphere is on the right and the gestalt is on the left. If you assess yourself by using the muscle checking guide, you will be able to tell if you have a transposed arrangement. Transposed learners are not specifically shown in this book. However, the same information can be gained by looking at profiles that are exactly opposite to your DomiKnow.

The only thing that won't hold true is the way the eye tracks information. Use your original dominant eye to determine the correct tracking pattern. No matter which hemisphere is gestalt or logic, the right eye will track from left to right while the left eye will track from right to left.

About the Profile Descriptions

In the pages that follow, each of the 32 basal Dominance Profiles is described. You will notice that a profile with a one letter name is followed by a profile with a double letter name. The difference between the two is simply that the one is right foot dominant, the other is left foot dominant. All other characteristics remain the same. The profiles are characterized by 1) which hemisphere is dominant in conditions of stress or when new learning is occurring, 2) the preferred functions or learning modalities in those situations, and 3) the functions which are limited under stress. Following that is a more detailed description of the characteristics of a learner with that profile. The "Helps" section which follows that is not meant to be an exhaustive list, but rather some suggestions which should point the way to behavior, habits, and practices which should prove beneficial to a learner with this profile. Additional information is presented in Chapter 4.

The Key on the facing page will help you to quickly find your profile.

Suppose, for example, your muscle checking or self-assessment reveals a dominance pattern like that of the boy illustrated on the cover of the book. Since he is gestalt *hemisphere* dominant, look first in the right column of the chart, under GESTALT HEMISPHERE DOMINANT. Then find the *hand,* in his case the left — the lower half of the column in the chart; then *eye* (his is left); then *ear* (his is right); then *foot* (his is right). His Dominance Profile is therefore Profile OO.

LOGIC HEMISPHERE DOMINANT

HAND	EYE	EAR	FOOT	PROFILE
Right Hand	Right Eye	Right Ear	Right Foot	A
			Left Foot	AA
		Left Ear	Right Foot	B
			Left Foot	BB
	Left Eye	Right Ear	Right Foot	C
			Left Foot	CC
		Left Ear	Right Foot	E
			Left Foot	EE
Left Hand	Right Eye	Right Ear	Right Foot	D
			Left Foot	DD
		Left Ear	Right Foot	F
			Left Foot	FF
	Left Eye	Right Ear	Right Foot	G
			Left Foot	GG
		Left Ear	Right Foot	H
			Left Foot	HH

GESTALT HEMISPHERE DOMINANT

HAND	EYE	EAR	FOOT	PROFILE
Right Hand	Right Eye	Right Ear	Right Foot	L
			Left Foot	LL
		Left Ear	Right Foot	J
			Left Foot	JJ
	Left Eye	Right Ear	Right Foot	K
			Left Foot	KK
		Left Ear	Right Foot	I
			Left Foot	II
Left Hand	Right Eye	Right Ear	Right Foot	PP
			Left Foot	P
		Left Ear	Right Foot	NN
			Left Foot	N
	Left Eye	Right Ear	Right Foot	OO
			Left Foot	O
		Left Ear	Right Foot	MM
			Left Foot	M

Figure 23: Key to the 32 Dominance Profiles

PROFILE A

Logic Dominant
All Sensory-Motor Modalities Available

* Learns best by focusing on the details. Processes by analysis, verbalization, and writing.

* Prefers structured learning and appreciates orderly sequencing of information.

* As both an auditory and visual learner, is able to pick up the details of information through the eyes and ears even under stress.

* Language (both oral and written) is very important for learning.

* Has the ability to follow step-by-step visual and auditory instructions, is able to follow specific written and verbal instructions and prefers directions to be precise and detailed.

* Needs to move when under stress or with new learning. Movements tend to be more planned (thinks before moving).

* Will prefer to sit on the right hand side of an auditorium or classroom in order to optimally access the right eye if more visually oriented or on the left side to access the right ear if more auditorily oriented.

* During stress, may have difficulty seeing the big picture ("can't see the forest for the trees").

* May find it challenging to connect to information emotionally or kinesthetically.

* Biggest challenge may be linear, piecemeal processing to the exclusion of the gestalt. Because the dominant hand, eye, ear and foot are all opposite

the logic hemisphere, this learner may have a very difficult time accessing the gestalt hemisphere when stressed.

*   When integrated, will be able to put the details in a more global context and more easily understand the emotions and communication of others, making relationships easier.

HELPS:

*   This learner especially should be encouraged to understand and synthesize information from a whole perspective, and explore ambiguity, emotions and movement.

*   Positive, enjoyable sensory-motor experiences will help develop the skills necessary to emotionally interact and fully access imagination, creativity and intuitive introspection.

*   An integrative balance of art, music, freeform movement and interpersonal/ intrapersonal skills combined with cognitive endeavors will be highly beneficial.

PROFILE AA

Logic Dominant
Functional: Visual, Auditory, Verbal
Limited Under Stress: Movement

* Learns best by focusing on the details. Processes by analysis, verbalization, and writing.

* Prefers structured learning and appreciates orderly sequencing of information.

* As both an auditory and visual learner, is able to pick up the details of information through the eyes and ears even under stress.

* Language (both oral and written) is very important for learning.

* Has the ability to follow step-by-step visual and auditory instructions.

* Under stress, may move forward with caution, feeling clumsy and stuck, or not move at all until they understand the situation. When relaxed, they prefer spontaneous, creative movement to structured movement when dancing.

* During stress, may have difficulty seeing the big picture ("can't see the forest for the trees").

* May find it challenging to connect to information emotionally or kinesthetically.

* Biggest challenge may be linear, piecemeal processing to the exclusion of the gestalt. Because the dominant hand, eye, and ear are all opposite the logic hemisphere, this learner may have a very difficult time accessing the gestalt hemisphere when stressed.

HELPS:

* This learner especially should be encouraged to understand and synthesize information from a whole perspective, and explore ambiguity, emotions and movement.

* Positive, enjoyable sensory-motor experiences will help develop the skills necessary to emotionally interact and fully access imagination, creativity and intuitive introspection.

* Integrated, cross-lateral foot movements like cross-crawl, walking, soccer, dancing, and martial arts (Tai Chi), Qi Gong, yoga, and pilates would be beneficial.

* An integrative balance of art, music, freeform movement and interpersonal/intrapersonal skills combined with cognitive endeavors will be highly beneficial.

PROFILE B

Logic Dominant
Functional: Visual, Verbal, Movement
Limited Under Stress: Auditory

* Learns best by focusing on the visual details. Processes by analysis, verbalization, and writing.

* Prefers structured learning and appreciates orderly sequencing of information.

* A visual learner that needs to see, speak and/or write in order to learn.

* Has the ability to follow step-by-step visual instructions. Enjoys structured dance steps.

* When fully integrated with both hemispheres on, they will prefer to listen to the tone, rhythm and emotional content of music and language. They will listen for the story and the metaphor.

* When the ear is limited during stress or with new learning, may have difficulty processing auditory input, especially detailed and specific information.

* May find it challenging to connect to visual information emotionally or kinesthetically.

* May have difficulty with memory, spelling and math skills due to temporal lobe/limbic connection with hearing and memory.

* Biggest challenge may be linear, piecemeal processing to the exclusion of the gestalt ("Can't see the forest for the trees").

HELPS:

*   Benefits from sitting at the front of the room on the right hand side to better access the dominant eye.

*   Encourage this person to understand and synthesize information from a whole perspective, and explore ambiguity, emotions and movement.

*   Positive, enjoyable sensory-motor experiences will help develop the skills necessary to emotionally interact and fully access imagination, creativity, and intuitive introspection.

*   Activities that help: reading out loud, active listening, Brain Gym Thinking Caps, Energy Yawn, the Owl, and the Elephant, listen to the lyrics of music and tone the vowel sounds.

*   An integrative balance of art, music, freeform movement and interpersonal/ intrapersonal skills combined with cognitive endeavors will be highly beneficial.

PROFILE BB

Logic Dominant
Functional: Visual, Verbal
Limited Under Stress: Auditory, Movement

* Learns best by focusing on the visual details. Processes by analysis, verbalization, and writing.

* Prefers structured learning and appreciates orderly sequencing of information.

* A visual learner that needs to see, speak and/or write in order to learn.

* Has the ability to follow step-by-step visual instructions.

* Under stress, may move forward with caution, feeling clumsy and stuck, or not move at all until they understand the details of the situation. If they do move, it may be clumsy and accidents may occur, especially to the right foot since it is not the dominant foot and as well organized. When relaxed, they prefer spontaneous, creative movement to structured movement when dancing.

* When fully integrated they prefer to listen to the emotions, story, metaphor, tone rhythm and global content of music and language.

* When the ear is limited during stress or with new learning, may have difficulty processing auditory input, especially detailed and specific information.

* May find it challenging to connect to visual information emotionally or kinesthetically.

* May have difficulty with memory, spelling and math skills due to temporal lobe/limbic connection with hearing and memory.

* Biggest challenge may be linear, piecemeal processing to the exclusion of the gestalt ("Can't see the forest for the trees").

HELPS:

* Benefits from sitting at the front of the room on the right hand side to better access the dominant eye.

* Encourage this person to understand and synthesize information from a whole perspective, and explore ambiguity, emotions and movement.

* Positive, enjoyable sensory-motor experiences will help develop the skills necessary to emotionally interact and fully access imagination, creativity, and intuitive introspection.

* Activities that help: reading out loud, active listening, Brain Gym Thinking Caps, Energy Yawn, the Owl, and the Elephant, listen to the lyrics of music and tone the vowel sounds.

* An integrative balance of art, music, freeform movement and interpersonal/ intrapersonal skills combined with cognitive endeavors will be highly beneficial.

PROFILE C

* Learns best by focusing on the auditory details. Processes by analysis, verbalization, and writing.

* Prefers structured learning and appreciates orderly sequencing of information.

* An auditory learner that needs to listen and explain either verbally or in writing to learn.

* Has the ability to follow step-by-step verbal instructions.

* Needs to move when under stress or with new learning. Movements tend to be more planned (thinks before moving).

* Left eye scans from right to left. Possible difficulty reading or writing languages that move from left to right like English. May reverse or transpose letters and/or numbers.

* When the left eye is limited during stress, the learner may need to close eyes in order to better access hearing, and may have difficulty seeing the specific details in visual information.

* Biggest challenge may be linear, piecemeal processing to the exclusion of the gestalt ("Can't see the forest for the trees").

* When relaxed, prefers to visually look for the big picture and emotional content and put it into a logical context to explain it.

HELPS:

* This person benefits from sitting on the left side a couple rows back to easily access their right ear.

* Encourage these people to understand and synthesize information from a whole perspective, and explore ambiguity, emotions and movement.

* Positive, enjoyable sensory-motor experiences will help develop the skills necessary to emotionally interact and fully access imagination, creativity, and intuitive introspection.

* Activities that help: movements that relax and use all eye muscles in an integrative way like Lazy 8's from Brain Gym, three dimensional art, blinking while tracking all around the edge of an object.

* An integrative balance of art, music, freeform movement and interpersonal/ intrapersonal skills combined with cognitive endeavors will be highly beneficial.

PROFILE CC

Logic Dominant
Functional: Auditory, Verbal
Limited Under Stress: Visual, Movement

* Learns best by focusing on the auditory details. Processes by analysis, verbalization, and writing.

* Prefers structured learning and appreciates orderly sequencing of information.

* An auditory learner that needs to listen and explain either verbally or in writing to learn.

* Has the ability to follow step-by-step verbal instructions.

* Under stress, may move forward with caution, feeling clumsy and stuck, or not move at all until they understand the situation. When relaxed, they prefer spontaneous, creative movement to structured movement when dancing.

* Left eye scans from right to left. Possible difficulty reading or writing languages that move from left to right like English. May reverse or transpose letters and/or numbers.

* When the left eye is limited during stress, the learner may need to close eyes in order to better access hearing, and may have difficulty seeing the specific details in visual information.

* When relaxed will visually look for the big picture and emotional content.

* Biggest challenge may be linear, piecemeal processing to the exclusion of the gestalt ("Can't see the forest for the trees").

HELPS:

* Benefits from sitting on the left side a couple rows back to easily access their right ear.

* Encourage these people to understand and synthesize information from a whole perspective, and explore ambiguity, emotions and movement.

* Positive, enjoyable sensory-motor experiences will help develop the skills necessary to emotionally interact and fully access imagination, creativity, and intuitive introspection.

* Activities that help: movements that relax and use all eye muscles in an integrative way like Lazy 8's from Brain Gym, three dimensional art, blinking while tracking all around the edge of an object. Also integrative cross-lateral foot play like cross-crawl, walking, soccer, dancing and martial arts like Tai Chi.

* An integrative balance of art, music, freeform movement and interpersonal/intrapersonal skills combined with cognitive endeavors will be highly beneficial.

PROFILE D

Logic Dominant
Functional: Visual, Auditory, Movement
Limited Under Stress: Verbal Communication

* Learns best by focusing on the visual/auditory details. Processes by analysis.

* Prefers structured learning and appreciates orderly sequencing of information.

* A visual/auditory learner that needs to see and hear the details in order to learn.

* Has the ability to follow step-by-step visual and verbal instructions.

* Needs to move when under stress or with new learning. Movements tend to be more planned (thinks before moving).

* With the dominant left hand connected to the kinesthetic gestalt hemisphere, may need to move, touch and manually explore in order to understand, organize and express information.

* When relaxed, may prefer to communicate the big picture and emotional context.

* Under stress may have difficulty communicating the details logically in a verbal or written way.

* Biggest challenge may be linear, piecemeal processing to the exclusion of the gestalt ("Can't see the forest for the trees").

HELPS:

* Will prefer to sit in the middle of a room to access both eye and ear, and in a space where they can doodle, or manipulate a pen or other object without bothering other people.

* Encourage this person to understand and synthesize information from a whole perspective, and explore ambiguity, emotions and movement.

* Positive, enjoyable sensory-motor experiences will help develop the skills necessary to emotionally interact and fully access imagination, creativity and introspection.

* Activities that help are: Integrated cross-lateral hand play like knitting, playing with clay, writing and drawing with both hands, and massaging the Temporal Mandibular Joint to assist communication.

* An integrative balance of art, music, freeform movement and interpersonal/intrapersonal skills combined with cognitive endeavors will be highly beneficial.

PROFILE DD

Logic Dominant
Functional: Visual, Auditory
Limited Under Stress: Verbal Communication, Movement

* Prefers structured learning and appreciates orderly sequencing of information.

* A visual/auditory learner that needs to see and hear the details in order to learn.

* Under stress, may move forward with caution feeling clumsy and stuck or not move at all until they understand the situation. When relaxed, they will prefer spontaneous, creative to structured, linear movements when dancing.

* With the dominant left hand connected to the kinesthetic gestalt hemisphere, may need to move, touch and manually explore in order to understand, organize and express information.

* When relaxed, may prefer to communicate the big picture and emotional context.

* Under stress may have difficulty communicating the details logically in a verbal or written way.

* Biggest challenge may be linear, piecemeal processing to the exclusion of the gestalt ("Can't see the forest for the trees").

HELPS:

* Will prefer to sit in the middle of the room to access both eye and ear in a space where they can doodle, or manipulate a pen or other object without bothering other people.

* Encourage these people to understand and synthesize information from a whole perspective, and explore ambiguity, emotions and movement.

* Positive, enjoyable sensory-motor experiences will help develop the skills necessary to emotionally interact and fully access imagination, creativity and introspection.

* Activities that help are: Integrated cross-lateral hand and foot play like knitting, playing with clay, writing and drawing with both hands, massaging the Temporal Mandibular Joint to assist communication, conscious walking, soccer, dancing and martial arts like Tai Chi.

* An integrative balance of art, music, freeform movement and interpersonal/ intrapersonal skills combined with cognitive endeavors will be highly beneficial.

PROFILE E

Logic Dominant
Functional: Verbal, Movement
Limited Under Stress: Visual, Auditory

*   Learns best by analyzing and communicating (either verbal or written), the details of information.

*   As a verbal learner, must talk about what is being learned in order to anchor it in and learn it.

*   Needs to move when under stress or with new learning. Movements tend to be more planned (thinks before moving).

*   Under stress or new learning may have difficulty seeing, hearing and remembering the details.

*   Left eye scans from right to left. Possible challenge reading or writing languages that move from left to right like English. May reverse or transpose letter and/or numbers.

*   May have difficulties following visual/auditory instructions, needing to talk through the instructions to understand them.

*   When relaxed, prefers to take in the whole picture and emotional context through the eyes and ears, and can then structure and sequence information in an orderly, logical way to explain it.

HELPS:

*   Will benefit from sitting further back where they can write and talk without disturbing others or by being a part of a cooperative learning group that has the freedom to talk to learn.

*   Activities that help: Lazy 8's for eyes, Vision Gym, Thinking Caps, and Energy Yawn from Brain Gym, blinking while tracking, Megaphones, listen for the lyrics and specific instruments in music.

*   An integrative balance of art, music, freeform movement and interpersonal/intrapersonal skills combined with cognitive endeavors will be highly beneficial.

PROFILE EE

Logic Dominant
Functional: Verbal
Limited Under Stress: Visual, Auditory, Movement

* Learns best by analyzing and communicating (either verbal or written), the details of information.

* As a verbal learner, must talk about what is being learned in order to anchor it in and learn it.

* Left eye scans from right to left. Possible challenge reading or writing languages that move from left to right like English. May reverse or transpose letter and/or numbers.

* Under stress may move forward with caution feeling clumsy and stuck, or not move until they understand the situation. When relaxed, they will prefer spontaneous, creative to structured linear movements when dancing.

* Under stress or new learning may have difficulty seeing, hearing and remembering the details.

* When relaxed prefers to to take in the whole picture and emotional context though the eyes and ears, and can then structure and sequence information in an orderly, logical way to explain to others.

* May have difficulties following visual/verbal instructions, needing to talk through the instructions to understand them.

HELPS:

*   Activities that help: Lazy 8's for eyes, Vision Gym, Thinking Caps from Brain Gym, blinking while tracking, Megaphones, Listening for the words of songs, integrated cross-lateral foot work like cross- crawls, walking, dancing, soccer, martial arts.

*   An integrative balance of art, music, freeform movement and interpersonal/ intrapersonal skills combined with cognitive endeavors will be highly beneficial.

PROFILE F

Logic Dominant
Functional: Visual, Movement
Limited Under Stress: Auditory, Verbal Communication

* Learns best by visually focusing on and analyzing the details of information.

* Prefers structured learning and appreciates orderly sequencing of visual information.

* As a visual learner must see the details in order to learn.

* Has the ability to follow visual step-by-step instructions.

* May see the details but have difficulty listening to, remembering, and then writing the details in an organized manner.

* Needs to move when under stress or with new learning. Movements tend to be more planned (thinks before moving).

* When relaxed prefers to listen to the tone, rhythm and emotional content of music and language.

* With the dominant left hand connected to the kinesthetic gestalt hemisphere, may need to move, touch and manually explore in order to organize and express information.

* When stressed will prefer not to talk. When relaxed, may prefer to communicate the big picture and emotional content through hand gestures.

* Biggest challenge may be linear, piecemeal processing to the exclusion of the gestalt.

HELPS:

*   Encourage this person to understand and synthesize information from a whole perspective, and explore ambiguity, emotions and movement.

*   Positive, enjoyable sensory-motor experiences will help develop the skills necessary to fully access imagination, creativity and introspection.

*   Will benefit from sitting in the front on the right hand side and being allowed to doodle or manipulate clay, a pen or other object.

*   Activities that help: reading out loud, active listening, Brain Gym Thinking Caps, megaphones, listening for the words of a song, and integrated cross-lateral hand play/work like knitting, writing and drawing with both hands, and massaging the Temporal Mandibular Joint to assist communication.

*   An integrative balance of art, music, freeform movement and interpersonal/intrapersonal skills combined with cognitive endeavors will be highly beneficial.

PROFILE FF

Logic Dominant
Functional: Visual
Limited Under Stress: Auditory, Verbal Communication, Movement

* Learns best by visually focusing on and analyzing the details of information.

* Prefers structured learning and appreciates orderly sequencing of visual information.

* May see the details but have difficulty listening to, remembering, and then writing the details in an organized manner.

* Under stress may move forward with caution feeling clumsy and stuck, or not move until they understand the situation. When relaxed, they will prefer spontaneous, creative to structured linear movements when dancing.

* When not under stress, enjoys listening to the tone, rhythm and emotional content of music and language.

* With the dominant left hand connected to the kinesthetic gestalt hemisphere, may need to move, touch and manually explore in order to organize and express information.

* When stressed will prefer not to talk. When relaxed, may prefer to communicate the big picture and emotional content through hand and body gestures.

* Biggest challenge may be linear, piecemeal processing to the exclusion of the gestalt.

HELPS:

* Encourage this person to understand and synthesize information from a whole perspective, and explore ambiguity, emotions and movement.

* Positive, enjoyable sensory-motor experiences will help develop the skills necessary to fully access imagination, creativity and introspection.

* This person will benefit from sitting in the front on the right hand side and being allowed to doodle or manipulate clay, a pen or other objects while learning.

* Activities that help: reading out loud, active listening, Brain Gym Thinking Caps, megaphones, listening for the words of a song, and integrated cross-lateral hand and foot play like knitting, writing and drawing with both hands, and massaging the Temporal Mandibular Joint to assist communication, conscious walking, dancing, soccer and martial arts like Tai Chi.

* An integrative balance of art, music, freeform movement and interpersonal/ intrapersonal skills combined with cognitive endeavors will be highly beneficial.

PROFILE G

Logic Dominant
Functional: Auditory, Movement
Limited Under Stress: Visual, Verbal Communication

* Learns best by focusing on auditory input and analyzing the details of information.
* Prefers structured learning and appreciates orderly sequencing of auditory information.
* As an auditory learner, must hear and usually has a good memory for the details, spelling and math.
* Has the ability to follow auditory step-by-step instructions.
* Needs to move when under stress or with new learning. Movements tend to be more planned (thinks before moving).
* Left eye scans from right to left. Possible challenge reading or writing languages that move from left to right like English. May reverse or transpose letter and/or numbers.
* May need to close eye and turn right ear toward information source with new learning or stressful information.
* With the dominant left hand connected to the kinesthetic gestalt hemisphere, may need to move, touch and manually explore in order to organize and express information.
* May have difficulty with penmanship and hand-eye coordination activities.
* When stressed will prefer not to talk. When relaxed, may prefer to communicate the big picture and emotional content through hand and body gestures.
* Biggest challenge may be linear, piecemeal processing to the exclusion of the gestalt.

HELPS:

* Encourage this person to understand and synthesize information from a whole perspective, and explore ambiguity, emotions and movement.

* Positive, enjoyable sensory-motor experiences will help develop the skills necessary to fully access imagination, creativity and introspection.

* Will benefit from sitting in the front of the room on the left hand side and being allowed to doodle or manipulate clay, a pen or other objects while learning.

* Activities that help: Lazy 8's for eyes, Vision Gym from Brain Gym, blinking while tracking, integrated cross-lateral hand play like knitting, writing and drawing with both hands, and massaging the Temporal Mandibular Joint to assist communication.

* An integrative balance of art, music, freeform movement and interpersonal/ intrapersonal skills combined with cognitive endeavors will be highly beneficial.

PROFILE GG

Logic Dominant
Functional: Auditory
Limited Under Stress: Visual, Verbal Communication, Movement

* Learns best by focusing on auditory input and analyzing the details of information.

* Prefers structured learning and appreciates orderly auditory sequencing of information.

* As an auditory learner must hear and usually has a good memory for the details, spelling and math.

* Under stress may move forward with caution feeling clumsy and stuck, or not move at all until they understand the situation. When relaxed they prefer creative and spontaneous to structured and linear movements when dancing.

* Left eye scans from right to left. Possible challenge reading or writing languages that move from left to right like English. May reverse or transpose letters and/or numbers.

* May need to close eyes and turn right ear toward information source with new learning.

* With the dominant left hand connected to the kinesthetic gestalt hemisphere, may need to move, touch and manually explore in order to organize and express information.

* May have difficulty with penmanship and hand-eye coordination activities.

* When stressed will prefer not to talk. When relaxed, may prefer to communicate the big picture and emotional content through hand gestures.

* Biggest challenge may be linear, piecemeal processing to the exclusion of the gestalt.

HELPS:

* Encourage this person to understand and synthesize information from a whole perspective, and explore ambiguity, emotions and movement.

* Positive, enjoyable sensory-motor experiences will help develop the skills necessary to fully access imagination, creativity and introspection.

* Will benefit from sitting in the front of the room on the left hand side and being allowed to doodle or manipulate clay, a pen or other object, while learning.

* Activities that help: Lazy 8's for eyes, Vision Gym from Brain Gym, blinking while tracking, integrated cross-lateral hand and foot play like knitting, writing and drawing with both hands, and massaging the Temporal Mandibular Joint to assist communication, conscious walking, dancing, soccer, and martial arts like Tai Chi.

* An integrative balance of art, music, freeform movement and interpersonal/ intrapersonal skills combined with cognitive endeavors will be highly beneficial.

PROFILE H

Logic Dominant
Functional: Movement
Limited Under Stress: Visual, Auditory, Verbal Communication

* Learns best by processing internally without external sensory stimulation. Quiet time alone is especially beneficial.

* Needs to move when under stress or with new learning. Movements tend to be more planned (thinks before moving).

* Left eye scans from right to left. Possible challenge reading or writing languages that move from left to right like English. May reverse or transpose letter and/or numbers.

* With the dominant eye and ear connected to the gestalt hemisphere, when relaxed, they prefer to see and hear the big picture/sound and emotional content.

* With the dominant left hand connected to the kinesthetic gestalt hemisphere, may need to move, touch and manually explore in order to organize and express information.

* May have difficulty with penmanship and hand-eye coordination activities.

* Seeing, hearing or communicating the details is often difficult, but when relaxed this person is often able to communicate the emotions and big picture via hand gestures.

* This almost totally left-limited profile means that under stress they are at a great disadvantage because at such times they cannot see or hear. However, when not stressed they can more easily see and hear the big picture and emotion — the gestalt — and put them into a logical context to express to others.

HELPS:

*   Will benefit from sitting where they can process internally, quietly and are allowed to doodle or manipulate clay, a pen or other object while learning.

*   Activities that help: Lazy 8's for Eyes, Vision Gym, Thinking Caps and the Elephant from Brain Gym, blinking while tracking, megaphone, integrated cross-lateral hand work like knitting, writing and drawing with the non-dominant hand, and massaging the Temporal Mandibular Joint to assist communication.

*   An integrative balance of art, music, freeform movement and interpersonal/intrapersonal skills combined with cognitive endeavors will be highly beneficial.

PROFILE HH

Logic Dominant

Limited Under Stress: All Modalities

* Learns best by processing internally without external sensory stimulation. Quiet time alone is especially beneficial.

* Under stress may move forward with caution feeling clumsy and stuck, or not move until they understand the situation. When relaxed they prefer creative and spontaneous to structured and linear movements when dancing.

* Left eye scans from right to left. Possible challenge reading or writing languages that move from left to right like English. May reverse or transpose letter and/or numbers.

* May have difficulty with penmanship and hand-eye coordination activities.

* With the dominant eye and ear connected to the gestalt hemisphere, when relaxed, they prefer to see and hear the whole context and emotions.

* With the dominant left hand connected to the kinesthetic gestalt hemisphere, may need to move, touch and manually explore in order to organize and express information.

* Seeing, hearing or communicating the details verbally is often difficult, but when relaxed this person is often able to communicate the emotions and whole context verbally and through hand gestures.

* This totally left-limited profile is at a great disadvantage when under stress because they cannot see, hear, move or communicate. However, when not stressed they can more easily see and hear the big picture and emotions — the gestalt — and put them into a logical context to express to others.

HELPS:

*   Will benefit from sitting where they can process internally, quietly and are allowed to doodle or manipulate clay, a pen or other object while learning.

*   Activities that help: Lazy 8's for eyes, Vision Gym, Thinking Caps and the Elephant from Brain Gym, blinking while tracking, megaphone, integrated cross-lateral hand and foot play like knitting, writing and drawing with both hands, and massaging the Temporal Mandibular Joint to assist communication, conscious walking, dancing, soccer, and martial arts like Tai Chi.

*   An integrative balance of art, music, freeform movement and interpersonal/ intrapersonal skills combined with cognitive endeavors will be highly beneficial.

PROFILE I

Gestalt Dominant
Functional: Visual, Auditory
Limited Under Stress: Verbal Communication, Movement

* A visual/auditory learner that must be able to see and hear the whole picture/sound and experience its emotional elements relevant to self in order to understand information and learn.

* Seeing and hearing the details will be difficult under stress.

* Interprets language primarily from its tone, pitch and rhythm (dialect).

* When relaxed can follow step-by-step instructions, though prefers to start by imagining the end results and then intuitively doing what seems appropriate.

* Under stress may move forward with caution feeling clumsy and stuck or not move at all until the situation feels safe to them. When relaxed, can follow structured dance steps.

* May have difficulty communicating verbally under stress. Will see the whole picture but not know where to start to chunk it down into the linear pieces of language to express it.

* When relaxed may be able to communicate the details and sequence of information, both verbally and in writing.

* Left eye scans from right to left. Possible challenge reading or writing languages that move from left to right like English. May reverse and/or transpose letters and/or numbers.

* Biggest challenge may be to access the pieces of information and be

able to put them together in a linear logical manner that they can then communicate.

HELPS:

* Encourage this person to relax before attempting to communicate the details and linear aspects of life and learning.

* Will benefit from sitting in the middle front of the room where they can access their dominant ear and eye.

* Activities that help: cross-lateral hand and foot play like knitting, writing and drawing with both hands, lazy 8's, energy yawn, cross crawls, walking, dancing, soccer and martial arts like Tai Chi, Yoga and Qi Gong.

* An integrative balance of art, music, movement and interpersonal skills combined with cognitive endeavors in linguistics and mathematics will be highly beneficial.

PROFILE II

Gestalt Dominant
Functional: Visual, Auditory, Movement
Limited Under Stress: Verbal Communication

* A visual/auditory learner that must be able to see and hear the whole picture/sound and experience its emotional elements relevant to self in order to understand and learn. Will have difficulties seeing and hearing the details when under stress.

* Interprets language primarily from its tone, pitch and rhythm (dialect).

* Has difficulty following step-by-step instructions, prefers to start by imagining the end results and then intuitively doing what seems appropriate.

* Needs to move when under stress or with new learning. Movements tend to be spontaneous and fluid — freeform, but the capacity to exhibit good technique (like a specific dance step) may deteriorate when stressed.

* May have difficulty communicating verbally under stress. Will see the whole picture but not know where to start to chunk it down into the linear pieces of language to express it.

* Left eye scans from right to left. Possible challenge reading or writing languages that move from left to right like English. May reverse and/or transpose letters and/or numbers.

* When relaxed may be able to communicate the details and sequence of information, both verbally and in writing.

* Biggest challenge may be to access the pieces of information and be able to put them together in a linear logical manner that they can then communicate.

HELPS:

* Encourage this person to relax before attempting to communicate the details and linear aspects of life and learning.

* Will benefit from sitting in the middle front of the room where they can access their dominant ear and eye.

* Activities that help: cross-lateral hand play like knitting, writing and drawing with both hands, Lazy 8's and energy yawn from Brain Gym.

* An integrative balance of art, music, movement and interpersonal skills combined with cognitive endeavors in linguistics and mathematics will be highly beneficial.

PROFILE J

Gestalt Dominant
Functional: Auditory
Limited Under Stress: Visual, Verbal Communication, Movement

* An auditory learner that must hear the story, metaphor and emotional elements relevant to self in order to understand and learn.

* Interprets language primarily from its tone, pitch and rhythm (dialect).

* Usually exhibits good memory for whole concepts or images.

* Because the eye is limited, may need to close the eyes and turn the left ear toward the sound when listening to and processing new information. When relaxed prefers to see the details.

* When relaxed can follow step-by-step instructions, though prefers to start by imagining the end results and then intuitively doing what seems appropriate.

* Under stress may move forward with caution feeling clumsy and stuck, or not move at all until the situation feels safe to them. When relaxed, can follow structured dance steps.

* May have difficulty communicating verbally under stress. Will see the whole picture but not know where to start to chunk it down into the linear pieces of language to express it.

* When relaxed may be able to communicate the details and sequence of information, both verbally and written.

* Biggest challenge may be to access the pieces of information and be able to put them together in a linear logical manner that they can then communicate.

HELPS:

* Encourage this person to relax before attempting to communicate the details and linear aspects of life and learning.

* Will benefit from sitting on the right side several rows back where they can hear easily.

* Activities that help: Lazy 8's from Brain Gym, blinking while tracking with the eyes, cross-lateral hand and foot play like knitting, writing and drawing with both hands, massaging the Temporal Mandibular Joint for communication, cross crawls, walking, dancing, soccer, martial arts like Tai Chi.

* An integrative balance of art, music, movement and interpersonal skills combined with cognitive endeavors in linguistics and mathematics will be highly beneficial.

PROFILE JJ

Gestalt Dominant
Functional: Auditory, Movement
Limited Under Stress: Visual, Verbal Communication

* An auditory learner must hear the story, metaphor and emotional elements relevant to self in order to understand and learn.

* Interprets language primarily from its tone, pitch and rhythm (dialect).

* Usually exhibits good memory for whole concepts or images.

* Because the eye is inhibited, may need to close the eyes and turn the left ear toward the sound when listening to and processing new information. When relaxed prefers to see the details.

* Has difficulty following step-by-step instructions, prefers to start by imagining the end results and then intuitively doing what seems appropriate.

* Needs to move when under stress or with new learning. Movements tend to be spontaneous and fluid — freeform, but the capacity to exhibit good technique (like a specific dance step) may deteriorate when stressed.

* May have difficulty communicating verbally under stress. Will see the whole picture but not know where to start to chunk it down into the linear pieces of language to express it.

* When relaxed may be able to communicate the details and sequence of information, both verbally and written.

* Biggest challenge may be to access the pieces of information and be able to put them together in a linear logical manner that they can then communicate.

HELPS:

* Encourage this person to relax before attempting to communicate the details and linear aspects of life and learning.

* Will benefit from sitting on the right side several rows back where they can hear easily.

* Activities that help: Lazy 8's from Brain Gym, blinking while tracking with the eyes, cross-lateral hand and foot play like knitting, writing and drawing with both hands, massaging the Temporal Mandibular Joint for communication, cross crawls, walking, dancing, soccer, martial arts like Tai Chi.

* An integrative balance of art, music, movement and interpersonal skills combined with cognitive endeavors in linguistics and mathematics will be highly beneficial.

PROFILE K

Gestalt Dominant
Functional: Visual
Limited Under Stress: Auditory, Verbal Communication, Movement

*   A visual learner that must see the whole three-dimensional perspective and emotional elements to learn.

*   When relaxed may hear and easily communicate the details and sequence of information, both verbally and in writing.

*   Under stress may move forward with caution, feeling clumsy and stuck, or not move at all until the situation feels safe to them. When relaxed, can follow structured dance steps.

*   May have difficulty communicating, listening and remembering when under stress. Will see the whole picture but not know where to start to chunk it down into the linear pieces of language to express it.

*   When relaxed can follow step-by-step instructions, though prefers to start by imagining the end results and then intuitively doing what seems appropriate.

*   Left eye scans from right to left. Possible challenge reading or writing languages that move from left to right like English. May reverse or transpose letters and/or numbers.

*   Biggest challenge may be to access the pieces of information and be able to put them together in a linear logical manner that they can then communicate.

HELPS:

* Encourage this person to relax before attempting to communicate the details and linear aspects of life and learning.

* Will benefit from sitting in the front row on the left hand side where they can access their left eye most easily.

* Activities that help: reading out loud, Thinking Caps and Cross Crawls from Brain Gym, megaphones, toning the vowels, and cross-lateral hand play like knitting, writing and drawing with both hands, and massaging the Temporal Mandibular Joint for communication,

* An integrative balance of art, music, movement and interpersonal skills combined with cognitive endeavors in linguistics and mathematics will be highly beneficial.

PROFILE KK

Gestalt Dominant
Functional: Visual, Movement
Limited Under Stress: Auditory, Verbal Communication

* A visual learner that must see the whole three-dimensional perspective and emotional elements to learn.

* Has difficulty following step-by-step instructions, prefers to start by imagining the end results and then intuitively doing what seems appropriate.

* Needs to move when under stress and with new learning. Movements tend to be spontaneous and fluid — freeform, but the capacity to exhibit good technique, like a specific dance, step may deteriorate when stressed.

* May have difficulty communicating, listening and remembering when under stress. Will see the whole picture but not know where to start to chunk it down into the linear pieces of language to express it.

* When relaxed may hear and easily communicate the details and sequence of information, both verbally and in writing.

* Left eye scans from right to left. Possible challenge reading or writing languages that move from left to right like English. May reverse or transpose letters and/or numbers.

* Biggest challenge may be to access the pieces of information and be able to put them together in a linear logical manner that they can then communicate.

HELPS:

* Encourage this person to relax before attempting to communicate the details and linear aspects of life and learning.

* Will benefit from sitting in the front row on the left hand side where they can access their left eye most easily.

* Activities that help: reading out loud, Thinking Caps from Brain Gym, megaphones, toning the vowels, and cross-lateral hand play like knitting, writing and drawing with both hands, and massaging the Temporal Mandibular Joint for communication.

* An integrative balance of art, music, movement and interpersonal skills combined with cognitive endeavors in linguistics and mathematics will be highly beneficial.

PROFILE L

Gestalt
Limited Under Stress: Receptive and Expressive Modalities

* Needs to process internally with minimal external sensory stimulus. Needs quiet time alone, especially when stressed or integrating new ideas. Will focus on the gestalt or whole picture and emotional relevance to self and other.

* Appreciates metaphors, examples and emotional associations when problem solving.

* When relaxed can follow step-by-step instructions, though prefers to start by imagining the end results and then intuitively doing what seems appropriate.

* Under stress may move forward with caution, feeling clumsy and stuck, or not move at all until the situation feels safe to them. When relaxed, can follow structured dance steps.

* May have difficulty communicating, seeing, listening and remembering when under stress. Will see the whole picture but not know where to start to chunk it down into the linear pieces of language to express it.

* When relaxed may see, hear and easily communicate the details and sequence of information, both verbally and in writing.

* Persons with this totally right-limited profile are at a great disadvantage when under stress because they cannot see, hear, move or communicate. This is the main profile seen in Special Education classes. Many of our most innovative thinkers have had this profile.

HELPS:

* Will benefit from sitting where they can process internally, quietly and move without disturbing other people. When relaxed, they prefer to be in the front where they can hear and see the details of information and write them down or discuss them.

* Activities that help: Lazy 8's and Thinking Caps from Brain Gym, blinking while tracking with the eyes, megaphones, integrated cross-lateral hand and foot play like knitting, writing and drawing with both hands, conscious walking, dancing, soccer, and martial arts like Tai Chi.

* An integrative balance of art, music, movement and interpersonal skills combined with cognitive endeavors in linguistics and mathematics will be highly beneficial.

PROFILE LL

Gestalt Dominant
Functional: Movement
Limited Under Stress: Visual, Auditory, Verbal Communication

* Needs to process internally with minimal external sensory stimulus. Needs quiet time alone, especially when stressed or integrating new ideas. Will focus on the gestalt or whole picture and emotional relevance to self and other.

* Appreciates metaphors, examples and emotional associations when problem solving.

* Has difficulty following step-by-step instructions, prefers to start by imagining the end results and then intuitively doing what seems appropriate.

* Needs to move when under stress or with new learning. Movements will be spontaneous and fluid — freeform, but the capacity to exhibit good technique, like a specific dance step may deteriorate when stressed.

* May have difficulty communicating, seeing, listening and remembering when under stress. Will see the whole picture but not know where to start to chunk it down into the linear pieces of language to express it.

* When relaxed may see, hear and easily communicate the details and sequence of information, both verbally and in writing.

* Persons with this profile are at a great disadvantage when under stress because they cannot see, hear or communicate. However, when relaxed, they prefer to see and hear the details and put them into a gestalt context which they can explain to others in an integrated logic/gestalt way. They have the ability to move forward with their ideas when involved and coherent.

PROFILE LL

HELPS:

* Will benefit from sitting where they can process internally, quietly and move without disturbing other people. When relaxed, they prefer to be in the front where they can hear and see the details of information and write them down or discuss them.

* Activities that help: Lazy 8's and Thinking Caps from Brain Gym, blinking while tracking with the eyes, megaphones, integrated cross-lateral hand play like knitting, writing and drawing with both hands, and massaging the Temporal Mandibular Joint for communication.

* An integrative balance of art, music, movement and interpersonal skills combined with cognitive endeavors in linguistics and mathematics will be highly beneficial.

PROFILE M

Gestalt Dominant
Full Sensory Access

* Learns best through movement and by focusing on the whole picture, context and emotional relevance to self.

* Must be able to see, hear, move and manually express the whole context before learning the details.

* Appreciates metaphors, examples and associations when problem solving. Looks and listens for the intention and emotion of the person and/or information.

* Interprets language primarily from its tone, pitch and rhythm (dialect).

* Learns kinesthetically, needing to move (especially the hands) to process new learning. Physically and emotionally expressive.

* Quickly grasps the main idea but may have great difficulty seeing, hearing and communicating the details in a linear way.

* Is often highly intuitive and prefers to process that way.

* Left eye scans from right to left. Possible difficulty reading or writing languages that move from left to right like English. May reverse or transpose letters and/or numbers.

* Has difficulty following step-by-step instructions. Tends to start by imagining the end results and then intuitively doing what seems appropriate.

* Needs to move when under stress and with new learning. Movements tend to be spontaneous and fluid — freeform, but the capacity to exhibit good technique (like a specific dance step) may deteriorate under stress.

* May have difficulty with penmanship. Benefits from fine-motor, hand-eye coordination play and work.

* Because the dominant hand, ear, eye and foot are all opposite the gestalt hemisphere, this person has no access to the logic hemisphere during new learning or when stressed. This person's biggest challenge will be to access the pieces of information, be able to put them together in a linear logical manner and communicate it verbally.

HELPS:

* Encouragement and good modeling on how to work with and communicate details and linear aspects of life and learning is very important.

* Will benefit from sitting toward the front but where they can move without disturbing other learners.

* Activities that help: any integrated cross-lateral movements like Lazy 8's, Thinking Caps, Cross-Crawl and Hook Ups from Brain Gym.

* An integrative balance of art, music, movement and interpersonal/ intrapersonal skills combined with cognitive endeavors in linguistics and mathematics will be highly beneficial.

PROFILE MM

Gestalt Dominant
Functional: Visual, Auditory, Kinesthetic Communication
Limited Under Stress: Movement

* Learns best by focusing on the whole picture, context and emotional relevance to self.

* Must be able to see, hear, and manually express the whole context before learning the details.

* Appreciates metaphors, examples and associations when problem solving. Looks and listens for the intention and emotion of the person and/or information.

* Interprets language primarily from its tone, pitch and rhythm (dialect).

* Learns kinesthetically, needing to move the hands in order to process new learning. Physically and emotionally expressive.

* Quickly grasps the main idea but may have great difficulty seeing, hearing and communicating the details in a linear way.

* Is often highly intuitive and prefers to process that way.

* Left eye scans from right to left. Possible difficulty reading or writing languages that move from left to right like English. May reverse or transpose letters and/or numbers.

* When not stressed can follow step-by-step instructions but prefers to start by imagining the end results and then intuitively doing what seems appropriate.

* Under stress may move forward with caution, feeling clumsy and stuck, or not move at all until the situations feels safe to them. When relaxed, can follow structured dance steps..

* May have difficulty with penmanship and hand-eye coordination. Benefits from fine-motor, hand-eye coordination play and work.

* Because the dominant hand, ear, and eye are all opposite the gestalt hemisphere, this person has almost no access to the logic hemisphere during new learning or when stressed. This person's biggest challenge will be to access the pieces of information, be able to put them together in a linear logical manner and communicate it.

HELPS:

* Encouragement and good modeling on how to work with and communicate details and linear aspects of life and learning is very important.

* Will benefit from sitting toward the front but where they can move their hands without disturbing other learners.

* Activities that help: any integrated cross-lateral movements like Lazy 8's, Cross-Crawl and Hook Ups from Brain Gym, walking, soccer, dancing and martial arts like Tai Chi.

* An integrative balance of art, music, movement and interpersonal/intrapersonal skills combined with cognitive endeavors in linguistics and mathematics will be highly beneficial.

PROFILE N

Gestalt Dominant
Functional: Auditory, Kinesthetic Communication, Movement
Limited Under Stress: Visual

* Learns best through movement and by focusing on the whole picture, context and emotional relevance to self.

* As an auditory/kinesthetic learner, processes by listening to the intention and emotion of the person and/or information and physically doing what is being learned.

* Appreciates metaphors, examples and associations when problem solving.

* Interprets language primarily from its tone, pitch and rhythm (dialect).

* Learns kinesthetically, needing to move (especially the hands) to process new learning. Physically and emotionally expressive.

* Quickly grasps the main idea but may have great difficulty hearing and communicating the details in a linear way.

* With the right eye blocked, may need to close the eyes and turn the dominant ear toward the sound when listening to information.

* Has difficulty following step-by-step instructions, prefers to start by imagining the end results and then intuitively doing what seems appropriate.

* When relaxed will prefer to look for the details.

* Needs to move when under stress and with new learning. Movements tend to be spontaneous and fluid — freeform, but the capacity to exhibit good technique (like a specific dance step) may deteriorate when stressed.

* Biggest challenge will be to access the pieces of information, be able to put them together in a linear logical manner and communicate it verbally.

HELPS:

* Encouragement and good modeling on how to work with and communicate details and linear aspects of life and learning is very important.

* Will benefit from sitting halfway back on the right side to access their hearing and where they can also move without disturbing others. Have them do something with their hands (clay, knitting, doodling) while listening to new learning.

* Activities that help: any integrated cross-lateral movements like Lazy 8's for eyes, cross crawl, three dimensional art, blinking while tracking around the edge of an object.

* An integrative balance of art, music, movement and interpersonal/ intrapersonal skills combined with cognitive endeavors in linguistics and mathematics will be highly beneficial.

PROFILE NN

Gestalt Dominant
Functional: Auditory, Kinesthetic Communication
Limited Under Stress: Visual, Movement

* Learns best through movement of the hand and by focusing on the whole picture, context and emotional relevance to self.

* As an auditory/kinesthetic learner, processes by listening to the intention and emotion of the person and/or information and physically doing what is being learned.

* Appreciates metaphors, examples and associations when problem solving.

* Interprets language primarily from its tone, pitch and rhythm (dialect).

* Learns kinesthetically, needing to move the hands in order to process new learning. Physically and emotionally expressive.

* Quickly grasps the main idea but may have great difficulty hearing and communicating the details in a linear way.

* With the right eye blocked, may need to close the eyes and turn the dominant ear toward the sound in a stressful situation or when learning new information.

* When relaxed will prefer to look for the details.

* When not stressed can follow step-by-step instructions. Prefers to start by imagining the end results and then intuitively doing what seems appropriate.

* Under stress may move forward with caution feeling clumsy and stuck, or not move at all until the situations feels safe to them. When relaxed, can follow structured dance steps.

* Biggest challenge will be to access the pieces of information, be able to put them together in a linear logical manner and communicate it.

HELPS:

* Encouragement and good modeling on how to work with and communicate details and linear aspects of life and learning is very important

* Will benefit from sitting halfway back on the right side to hear but where they can also move without disturbing other learners. Have them do something with their hands (clay, knitting, doodling) while listening to new learning.

* Activities that help: any integrated cross-lateral movements like Lazy 8's for eyes, cross crawl, three dimensional art, blinking while tracking around the edge of an object, soccer, martial arts like Tai Chi.

* An integrative balance of art, music, movement and interpersonal/ intrapersonal skills combined with cognitive endeavors in linguistics and mathematics will be highly beneficial.

PROFILE O

Gestalt Dominant
Functional: Visual, Kinesthetic Communication, Movement
Limited Under Stress: Auditory

* Learns best through movement and by focusing on the whole picture, context and emotional relevance to self.

* As a visual/kinesthetic learner must see the whole picture and physically do what is being learned.

* Appreciates metaphors, examples and associations when problem solving.

* Learns kinesthetically, needing to move (especially the hands) to process new learning. Emotionally and physically expressive.

* Visually grasps the main idea but may have great difficulty seeing and communicating the details in a linear way.

* When relaxed may preferentially listen for the details.

* Left eye scans from right to left. Possible difficulty reading or writing languages that move from left to right like English. May reverse or transpose letters or numbers.

* Has difficulty following step-by-step instructions, prefers to start by imagining the end results and then intuitively doing what seems appropriate.

* May have difficulty with penmanship because the eye and hand don't work together. Benefits from fine-motor, hand-eye coordination activities.

* Needs to move when under stress and with new learning. Movements tend to be spontaneous and fluid— freeform, but the capacity to exhibit good technique (like a specific dance step) may deteriorate under stress.

* Biggest challenge will be to access the pieces of information, be able to put them together in a linear logical manner and communicate it berbally.

HELPS:

* Encouragement and good modeling on how to work with and communicate details and linear aspects of life and learning is very important

* Will benefit from sitting close to the front on the left hand side to access their left eye but where they can also move without disturbing others.

* Activities that help: Lots of movement, reading out loud, Thinking Caps from Brain Gym, megaphones, toning the vowels and hand-eye coordination play like Lazy 8's for writing, double doodles.

* An integrative balance of art, music, movement and interpersonal/ intrapersonal skills combined with cognitive endeavors in linguistics and mathematics will be highly beneficial.

PROFILE OO

Gestalt Dominant
Functional: Visual, Kinesthetic Communication
Limited Under Stress: Auditory, Movement

* Learns best through movement of the hands and by focusing on the whole picture, context and emotional relevance to self.

* As a visual/kinesthetic learner must see the whole picture and physically do what is being learned.

* Appreciates metaphors, examples and associations when problem solving.

* Visually grasps the main idea but may have great difficulty seeing and communicating the details in a linear way.

* When relaxed may preferentially listen for the details.

* Left eye scans from right to left. Possible difficulty reading or writing languages that move from left to right like English. May reverse or transpose letters or numbers.

* When not stressed can follow step-by-step instructions. Prefers to start by imagining the end results and then intuitively doing what seems appropriate.

* May have difficulty with penmanship because the eye and hand don't work together. Benefits from fine-motor, hand-eye coordination activities.

* Under stress may move forward with caution feeling clumsy and stuck, or not move at all until the situation feels safe to them. When relaxed, can follow structured dance steps.

* Biggest challenge will be to access the pieces of information, be able to put them together in a linear logical manner and communicate it verbally.

HELPS:

* Encouragement and good modeling on how to work with and communicate details and linear aspects of life and learning is very important

* Will benefit from sitting close to the front on the left hand side but where they can also move without disturbing other learners.

* Activities that help: lots of movement, reading out loud, Thinking Caps from Brain Gym, megaphones, toning the vowels and hand-eye coordination play like Lazy 8's for writing, double doodles. and integrated cross-lateral foot play like cross crawl, walking, soccer, dancing and martial arts like Tai Chi.

* An integrative balance of art, music, movement and interpersonal/ intrapersonal skills combined with cognitive endeavors in linguistics and mathematics will be highly beneficial.

PROFILE P

Gestalt Dominant
Functional: Kinesthetic Communication, Movement
Limited Under Stress: Visual, Auditory

* Learns best through movement and by focusing on the whole picture, context and emotional relevance to self.

* Learning must be processed through movement, emotion and intuition. Needs to physically do what is being learned.

* Especially needs to move the hands to process new learning. Physically and emotionally expressive.

* Appreciates metaphors, examples and associations when problem solving.

* Because both eye and ear are blocked, needs time alone to process internally without visual or auditory stimulation when stressed.

* When relaxed will preferentially look and listen for the details, but have difficulty communicating them in a linear logical way either verbally or through writing.

* Has difficulty following step-by-step instructions, prefers to start by imagining the end results and then intuitively doing what seems appropriate.

* Needs to move when under stress and with new learning. Movements tend to be spontaneous and fluid — freeform, but the capacity to exhibit good technique, like a specific dance step may deteriorate under stress.

* Biggest challenge will be to access the pieces of information, be able to put them together in a linear logical manner and communicate it verbally.

HELPS:

* Encouragement and good modeling on how to work with and communicate details and linear aspects of life and learning is very important

* Will benefit from sitting at the back of the room where they can move without disturbing others. They will need to be moving their hands with clay, knitting or doodling during learning.

* Activities that help: Lots of movement, Lazy 8's and Thinking Caps from Brain Gym, blinking while tracking with the eyes, megaphones, reading out loud, and cross-lateral hand play like knitting, writing and drawing with the non-dominant hand, and massaging the Temporal Mandibular Joint for communication.

* An integrative balance of art, music, movement and interpersonal/ intrapersonal skills combined with cognitive endeavors in linguistics and mathematics will be highly beneficial.

PROFILE PP

Gestalt Dominant
Functional: Kinesthetic Communication
Limited Under Stress: Visual, Auditory, Movement

* Especially needs to work with the hands, physically doing what is being presented in order to learn it.

* Because both eye and ear are blocked, needs time alone to process internally without visual or auditory stimulation when stressed.

* Appreciates metaphors, examples and associations when problem solving.

* May be able to follow step-by-step visual and auditory instructions when relaxed but tends to start by imagining the end results and then intuitively doing what seems appropriate.

* When relaxed will preferentially look and listen for the details, but have difficulty communicating them in a linear logical way either verbally or through writing.

* Under stress may move forward with caution feeling clumsy and stuck, or not move at all until the situation feels safe to them. When relaxed, can follow structured dance steps.

* Biggest challenge will be to access the pieces of information, be able to put them together in a linear logical manner and communicate it.

* According to researchers working with Albert Einstein's brain, and written observations regarding his life, this is thought to be the Albert Einstein profile.

HELPS:

* Encouragement and good modeling on how to work with and communicate details and linear aspects of life and learning is very important

* Will benefit from sitting at the back of the room where they can move without disturbing other learners. They will need to be moving their hands with clay, knitting or doodling during learning.

* Activities that help: Lots of movement, Lazy 8's and Thinking Caps from Brain Gym, blinking while tracking with the eyes, megaphones, reading out loud, and cross-lateral hand and foot play like knitting, writing and drawing with the non-dominant hand, massaging the Temporal Mandibular Joint for communication, cross crawl, walking, dancing, soccer and martial arts like Tai Chi.

* An integrative balance of art, music, movement and interpersonal/intrapersonal skills combined with cognitive endeavors in linguistics and mathematics will be highly beneficial.

❧ 4 ❦

Getting It All Together

Ideally, we all expand our capacities beyond our basal profiles and learn to use both brain hemispheres well, to use our eyes, our ears, and movements of our hands and feet to full capacity. When we learn and perform in whole-brained, integrated ways we achieve more, developing more varied skills and competencies. It is possible to become more logical and analytical (logic hemisphere) or to become more imaginative and intuitive (gestalt hemisphere). We can learn verbal communication skills or increase our kinesthetic abilities. We can increase our visual skills or become better at listening.

As we grow and become schooled, we have opportunities to develop compensatory strategies for learning and most of us do pick up a thing or two over the years to help us work better. This chapter will offer some ideas that you and/or the people in your life may not have learned which may further encourage whole-brain integration. Many of the suggestions are physical movements and other widely used techniques that have been found to assist brain integration. Many come from the Brain Gym® work put together from many modalities by Paul and Gail Dennison. Other practices are widely used techniques found in many different books about learning. If a technique is unfamiliar to you, look for it in Appendix B where you will find an alphabetical listing of learning techniques and sources, with more detailed descriptions.

How To Be More Whole-Brained —
Help for the Gestalt Dominant Learner

If you are gestalt dominant in your basal profile, there are many habits and strategies that will help you to become more orderly and analytical in your thinking, creativity and work habits. After all, everyone does have a logic hemisphere, and even if it's not your inclination to do so, you *are* able to make lists, prioritize, classify, sequence, arrange things in order alphabetically, numerically and hierarchically. Logic hemisphere thinking has many advantages. Logic processing allows you to reason and make judgments based on objective measurements and logical thought patterns. Logic brain checks and measurements can help steer you away from wild goose chases and pie in the sky projects.

If you are gestalt hemisphere dominant, your tendency is to see the big picture and to be less concerned with the details. The trouble with this inclination is that without the details the rest of the world may not know what you are talking about. The challenge for you is to break down your intuitive grasp of things into manageable, identifiable pieces that can be organized and then explained or proven to the rest of us. Using logic hemisphere strategies like math, sequencing of steps, flow-charting, outlining, etc., will help you to communicate your knowledge and great insights to others.

The scientific method with its emphasis on controlled, strictly measured testing of a hypothesis is a good example of integrated functioning. Gestalt hemisphere processes inspire a hypothesis, then logic hemisphere processes test the theory in an objective way, thereby increasing the chance that a true picture emerges from the test.

Strategies and Habits for Gestalt Hemisphere Learners

- *Make lists*
- *Prioritize*
- *Sequence and use Flow Charts*
- *Attend to details*

- *Learn Time Management*
- *Force yourself to finish what you start*
- *Use objective measurements — quantify, use statistics*
- *Analyze decisions and go through logical reasoning processes*
- *List advantages and disadvantages of a decision and rate each on a scale of 1-10 to give a numerical rating*
- *Break large concepts into smaller pieces. Use outlines, draw pictures, make mind maps to clarify relationships between the pieces of information*
- *Write poems or songs that rhyme and have a numerical sequence*
- *Memorize information using mnemonics, set the information to a tune you know, or make up your own song, repeat or sing the information while jumping on a rebounder or while walking,*
- *Practice observing detail with line drawings or drafting*
- *Practice sequencing when you communicate: "There are three points to this discussion: One, ..."*
- *Study the detail of a plant or other natural object*
- *Force yourself to read and follow directions (e.g., computer instructions)*
- *Study the time and use a metronome when playing or singing music*

Help for the Logic Dominant Learner

If you are logic dominant in your basal profile you may have to develop habits that encourage your gestalt hemisphere processing. Crucial insights, novel ideas, artistic inspirations, empathy and altruism originate in the emotion-based, image-making gestalt hemisphere, so does intuitive understanding. If you are logic dominant you may need to acquire habits that help spark this image-making capacity, understanding and empathizing with others, and learning to trust your intuition and emotions.

Allow time and space for idea generation. Inspiration is not methodical. Great ideas often spring from unconscious processes that may surface out of the blue, days after you start working on a problem or task. If you have a tendency to censor and dismiss your ideas too quickly, you can develop loosening up strategies like brainstorming, or creative visualization. These techniques prime your brain's unconscious processes to tie memories or associations together in new ways, sometimes yielding exciting combinations.

When making decisions, learn to trust intuitive knowledge or hunches. Sometimes problems defy logical analysis, and research shows that a high percentage of first hunches are best and most accurate. Complex problems may have variables that are difficult to relate and quantify. In such cases it often helps to follow intuitive feelings or instincts to find solutions. In many cases people intuitively know the answer and only afterward break it down with logical analysis to explain it to other people or to verify the insights.

If you are logic hemisphere dominant you may also need to encourage your emotional expression. Put aside those tired, worn out prejudices we all learned about not "being too emotional." Emotions are energy in motion and constitute our motivation and passion for life, the cornerstones of relationships, leading us to understanding, compassion and interconnectedness. Emotional content is essential in all creative endeavors and in most avenues of communication from sales pitches to book length essays. Physical movement can help you develop expressiveness and bring you out of your tendency toward detail.

Strategies and Habits for Logic Dominant Learners

- *Brainstorm*
- *Visualize unusual images in your mind's eye*
- *Use picture and symbol mind maps (as opposed to outlines) for more fluid idea generation*
- *Pay more attention to gut instincts — trust your intuition*
- *Be aware of your emotions and express them — especially spontaneous joy*
- *Be physically active, especially with highly integrative, non-competitive activities*

— such as hiking, swimming, yoga, Qi Gong, Tai Chi and Brain Gym®
- *Learn to accept and be comfortable with ambiguity and paradox*
- *Write poems and songs that contain rich images and don't rhyme*
- *Use metaphors and emotional stories whenever possible*
- *Practice saying things in new ways ("In other words . . .")*
- *Talk more slowly using fewer words*
- *Play with impressionistic and free-form color painting, sculpture and dance*
- *Role-play business or personal situations to understand the big picture*

Integration in Creative Pursuits

Below is a chart of some common creative pursuits and the logic and gestalt hemisphere functions that are involved in their practice. If you wish to improve your creative output, you need to check both sides of the chart.

	LOGIC	GESTALT
ART	What media to use	Image
	How to show perspective	Emotion
	How to blend colors	Rhythm
	Techniques for using brush,	Spontaneity
	pallet knife, pens, pencils, etc.,	Intuition
	for greatest effect	
MUSIC	Techniques for playing the instrument	Image
	How to read the notes	Emotion
	Awareness of key signature and timing	Rhythm
	How to use the vocal folds	Spontaneity
	for a specific sound	Intuition

DANCE	Ballet positions for stability	Emotion
	Specific dance steps	Image
	Choreography	Rhythm
	How to move the eyes	Spontaneity
	to maintain balance	Intuition
SPORTS	Rules of the game	Whole picture
	Techniques for using the equipment	Rhythm
	How to move the body for	Spontaneity
	stability	Passion for the sport

When I learned to play the violin I had to engage both hemispheres and all of my senses. At first, my lessons were more logic-oriented, involving notes, timing, how to hold the violin and bow, watching the progression of notes and listening for specific tones. As I progressed, the violin became an emotional extension of my passion for life and music, engaging my gestalt hemisphere with the learned technique so I could truly create something wonderful.

Current research on the brain shows that people who play musical instruments, especially complicated ones like the violin, have more integrative nerve pathways. The same is true of art, theater, dance and sports. In order to truly excel in all these endeavors, there must be an integration of the technique (logic hemisphere) with the passion, image, story and personal emotion you bring to the art form (gestalt hemisphere).

Physical Movement Increases Brain Integration

One of the best ways to get the two sides of the brain working together is to engage in cross-lateral physical movement. What do I mean by the term cross-lateral?

Those movements where limbs on one side of the body cross the body's midline and coordinate with limbs on the other side of the body — so that both sides of the brain are being used at once. When playing the violin, I have to move my left fingers on the strings to produce the notes, while my right arm crossed my midline, moving the bow across the strings to produce the sound. Cross-lateral movements actually improve the nerve communication between the two sides of the brain.

For years we have known about the formative value of crawling in early childhood. This early cross-lateral activity is crucial for setting up neural links between the two brain hemispheres. Children who miss or shortchange the crawling stage are likely to have learning difficulties later on. Cross-lateral movements have been found to stimulate the growth of new nerve cells and BDNF (Brain Derived Nerve Growth Factor) that facilitates learning and memory throughout life.[19] They are among the best prescriptions for people with unilateral profiles for eyes, ears, hands and/or feet.

This notion of moving the body to help you learn better is new and startling to many people. If it seems surprising to you, consider what happens when you perform physical movements. You are not only using your bones and muscles — you are also using nerve pathways in the brain and between the brain and the rest of the body. The neural pathways you use to move your arm in a cross-lateral exercise include many of the same pathways you would use to write with or gesture with in learning activities. The more you stimulate these neural pathways by using them, the more efficiently they work, for all activities.

The same is true of muscles you use for speaking, seeing, hearing, touching, etc. All of our senses work by using muscles. There are specialized muscles in our eyes and ears. Muscles move our hands for touching, our tongues and noses for tasting and smelling. We cannot see, hear, touch, taste, smell or get a sense of our body's position (this last item on the list is a sensory system that we call proprioception) without moving muscles. And whenever we are moving muscles, we are stimulating and building up nerve pathways too — pathways that help us perform all sorts of tasks.

As I mentioned before, cross-lateral movements are especially helpful to brain and sensory integration. There are even cross-lateral exercises for the eyes that you may find helpful. (Sources are listed in Appendix B.)

Other kinds of movements are beneficial to the learning process as well, especially movements that stimulate the vestibular system, considered the entryway into the brain because it wakes up the brain and maintains alertness to incoming stimuli. This sensory-motor system connects the semicircular canals of the inner ear with the brain stem, eyes and core muscles, thus it regulates our balance for such activities as walking, skipping, standing on one foot, hopping and eventually using a pencil or pen to write with. It is an important component of the brain's ability to maintain alertness. Science is proving that we must move to learn.

Walking, which coordinates arms and legs together, is an all-around good activity for stimulating the brain. Knitting, which involves skilled movements of the hands in concert, is another good example. I once had a student in an anatomy and physiology course who sat in the back of the room and knitted during the whole class. She never took a note and very seldom looked at me. She got one of the highest grades in the course, and knitted nine sweaters that semester! She was an auditory learner, and did not need to look at me or the board to learn. And, by using both hands while knitting, she was accessing both hemispheres and keeping them equally activated.

The most important activity we can engage in to increase brain integration is unstructured, imaginative play, so crucial for social, emotional and cognitive development. For children creative play is critical to becoming socially adept, coping with stress and building cognitive skills such as problem solving. For adults it is critical for coping with stress and becoming more open and creative.[20]

Following are some good ideas to get you moving in brain stimulating ways. If you are interested in knowing more about the role of movement in learning I refer you to my book, *Smart Moves, Why Learning Is Not All In Your Head*, which explores the subject in much more depth.

Brain Beneficial Movements Menu

- *Take a walk. Start out fast and then slow down so that every cross movement of the walk becomes very conscious.*
- *Do Tai Chi, Yoga, gymnastics or cross-lateral aerobics.*
- *Do Brain Gyms®, especially Cross Crawl, Elephants, Lazy 8's and Hook Ups, slowly with balance*
- *Dance, play a musical instrument or sing*
- *Knit, play with clay or plasticine*
- *Hug wrestle with your kids, pets, mate — rough-and-tumble play[21]*
- *Climb a tree, do a ropes course*
- *Walk across a narrow bridge, balance beam or tightrope*
- *Swim, ski, skate, and surf*
- *Play cross-lateral games like: tennis, soccer, volley ball*
- *Take time to be quiet by yourself and even daydream[22, 23]*

The Eyes — Help for Homolateral (Limited) Vision

A visually limited profile will affect your ability to take in visual information. Reading, especially in stressful circumstances, may be a problem. Under stress, the eyes tend to move outward, relying on a broad, peripheral focus in order to see where the danger is. This makes convergent eye teaming difficult, and therefore reading. Because your primary function is survival, if asked to read when stressed, the dominant eye will be looking for danger and you will read with your non-dominant eye. This causes comprehension to decrease. Also, because your dominant eye is opposite the non-dominant hemisphere, which is shut down during stress, visual information is greatly decreased.

There are a number of physical activities that will increase your ability to take in visual information. Some are stress reducers and others are cross-lateral activities that use both sets of eye muscles, sensory information from both eyes, and both sides of the brain together thereby increasing integration.

- *Do Brain Gyms®, especially Brain Buttons, Lazy 8's for eyes, Energy Yawn and Vision Gym*
- *Cross your eyes*
- *Move your eyes in all visual fields, dancing them around the room*
- *Blink while tracking all around the edge of an object with both eyes*
- *Look at Magic Eye picture books to see the hidden forms*
- *Breathe deeply and rest your eyes on pastel colors or on a landscape in the distance with lots of blues and greens*
- *Take a walk in nature, letting your eyes gently lead you*
- *Practice visualizing colors, unusual patterns and thinking visually*
- *Develop a keen sense of observation by looking from very small objects to the whole picture — back and forth several times and then recall what you saw*
- *Take eye time outs and just shut and rest your eyes*
- *Follow a graceful hand dance with your eyes*

The Ears — Help for Homolateral (Limited) Hearing

If you have a limited auditory profile (both the dominant ear and hemisphere are on the same side), the following suggestions will help increase your intake of auditory information by decreasing stress and accommodating both ears and both hemispheres working together.

- *Do Brain Gyms®, especially Thinking Caps and The Owl*
- *Practice active listening with a partner, repeating back what they have said*
- *Tone the vowels (A, E, I, O, U) by taking in a deep breath and saying the vowel in a long sustained manner as you breathe out. More benefit is gained if you*

use the whole mouth, full breath, and relax so the sound comes out more as a tone that vibrates

- *In order for children to easily learn symbolic language, say the noun first so they can focus on the object and then add the qualifier: "The balloon is red" rather than "the red balloon."[24]*

- *Listen to 60 beat per minute music — the largo and adagio movements of Baroque music*

- *Read stories out loud with a lot of expression, tone changes and foreign dialects*

- *Sing a lot, by yourself or in groups*

- *Make "rabbit ears" by putting your fingers behind your ears, pulling them forward and listen to yourself talk.*

- *Practice listening for tonal patterns, pitch, melody and rhythms in music and in voices — your own and others*

- *Tap out the rhythm of your speech pattern and that of others*

- *Be very quiet and listen for your heart beat, the sounds of air molecules hitting your ear drums, and the silences between sounds.*

- *Reach out with your hearing as far as you can to pick up distant sounds*

- *Spend time in the dark without vision, forcing your hearing to become more acute.*

The Hands — Help for Homolateral (Limited) Communication or (Limited) Kinesthetic Manipulation

If your dominant hand and dominant hemisphere are on the same side (limited), there are a number of ways to achieve more integrated functioning and thus be more adept at using your hands. These activities will help you to communicate better verbally, through writing and with gestures. They will also help you to manipulate objects better for doing skilled work. Explore the following suggestions:

- *Do Brain Gyms®, especially Lazy 8's for writing and Double Doodles, on a stimulating surface like a rug, rough wall, in rice or on fine sandpaper. This stimulates both the sensory and motor cortexes for the hand and auditory areas of the brain*
- *Knit, do sculpture, play with clay*
- *Consciously move each finger of both hands in all directions*
- *Do finger mirror dances by putting the fingertips of both hands together and move them to music*
- *Practice communicating only with your hands*
- *Play a musical instrument, type, do beadwork or anything else that requires conscious, fine motor coordination of the hands*
- *Throw a ball with alternate hands*
- *Write and draw with your non-dominant hand*
- *Use large expressive arm movements in all directions*

And since speaking is directly associated with the hands, do the following activities as well:

- *Massage the Temporal Mandibular Joint (where the lower jaw articulates with the upper jaw, just in front of the ears) and the muscles surrounding your jaws. This activates sensory and motor nerves that assist vocalization*
- *Intone the vowel sounds while opening and closing the mouth in all different ways. Tone the vowels (A, E, I, O, U) by taking in a deep breath and saying the vowel in a long sustained manner as you breathe out. More benefit is gained if you use the whole mouth, full breath, and relax so the sound comes out more as a tone that vibrates.*

- *Talk gibberish with someone, making odd sounds and facial expressions using all the various emotions*
- *Sing a lot and do Mock Opera for fun*

The Feet — Help for Homolateral (Limited) Foot Coordination

You can increase coordination in your feet with the following suggestions:

- *Go barefoot as often as possible, especially on varied surfaces, to stimulate both feet and therefore both hemispheres*
- *Do Brain Gyms®, especially Cross Crawls and moving forward, backward and in circles while doing Hook Up's. This can also be done with eyes closed*
- *Take a walk starting out fast then slowing down until every movement is very conscious*
- *Do cross-lateral footwork, especially dancing, soccer, martial arts*
- *Practice leading with your non-dominant foot*
- *Do mirror movements with both feet where each foot does just the opposite action of the other foot*

Waking Up All the Senses

Give yourself a massage using all kinds of touch, especially to the hands and lips where there are more sensory receptors. This suggestion stems from Jean Ayer's work on sensory-motor integration. The varied pressure massage has a profound effect on waking up the whole system to efficiently take in and process information. In learning situations with both adults and children, take a wake-up break. Do it even if you're working alone. An activity that I have used incorporates hand movements to a story about a mouse, a cat and the rain.

First use light touch on yourself as the mouse runs (use your fingertips) all over the arms and especially around and through the finger forest of the opposite hand. Then comes the cat with solid pressure all along both arms and hands. And just when the cat is getting close to the mouse, here comes the wind (making whooshing sounds while brushing the arms), and then comes the rain (fingertips tapping raindrops over both arms and hands). It gets so soggy that the mouse runs to the legs and all around the toes. Then the cat comes stomping along the legs with solid pressure, and the wind and finally the rain comes with its tapping raindrops on the legs. Then the mouse runs up to and all around the head, especially around the lips followed by the cat, the wind, and the rain.

This wakes up all the sense receptors in key areas, especially the fingers and lips that have more sensory receptors, and activates fine motor function. The touch also stimulates the production of BDNF (Brain Derived Nerve Growth Factor) increasing dendritic growth of neurons for enhanced learning. Encourage children to come up with sensory-motor play stories that the whole group can participate in.[25, 26]

Seating Arrangements in Classrooms

This may not be an item that you or your child can practically arrange, but if you do have a chance to choose your seat in a classroom or office space, make sure it is one that facilitates your Dominance Profile. If you are a visual learner, make sure you sit up in the front of the classroom, preferably with right eye dominant on the right-hand side of the room and left eye dominant on the left-hand side. Auditory learners can sit anywhere they can hear well, but if left ear dominant, sit on the right side of the classroom, and if right ear dominant, sit on the left side of the room. If you are a kinesthetic learner, you may sit anywhere, but preferably where you won't disturb other learners with your moving. Optimally, have some clay or other quiet material to handle or doodle with while learning.

But You Need Stress Reduction Too

Stress is the main culprit in keeping you in your basal profile, unable to use both hemispheres and all of your senses. Even if you've learned compensations and adaptive strategies, they will disappear in stressful circumstances. Suddenly, you may not see as well or hear as well. You may have trouble communicating or become clumsy. You may become too linear in your thinking or want to physically withdraw from the situation. However, you can learn to function better and develop competencies beyond your basal profile's when you reduce and counteract stress. Many of the techniques we mentioned for brain integration will also reduce tension levels in the body and help you to dissipate stress.

Here are some things you can do to alleviate stress:

- *Do Hook Up's while focusing on breathing and being absolutely present*
- *Take a conscious walk — preferably in nature*
- *Do Brain Gyms® Elephants, Energy Yawn, Yoga, Tai Chi, Qi Gong*
- *Dance, sing, hum or whistle*
- *Play a musical instrument*
- *Hug wrestle with your kids, pets, mate*

If you're in a situation where you can't move the whole body:

- *Do Brain Gyms®, especially Hook Ups and Lazy 8's*
- *Drink lots of water*
- *Breathe slowly and deeply to release the tension in your muscles*
- *Hold your forehead lightly until you feel a pulse under your hands*
- *Knit, play with clay or plasticine*

- *Draw or doodle a picture using both hands at the same time*
- *Listen to integrative music (classical, complex sustained rhythms in African and South American music)*
- *Focus on a positive aspect of the situation, perhaps what lessons you are learning from the experience*
- *Find the humor of the situation*
- *Intentionally be present, focusing on your surroundings and what you are grateful for*

✳ 5 ✳

Dominance Profiles in Human Relationships

It takes all kinds to make a world. It even seems to take all kinds to make just one family — and without a doubt, it takes all kinds of patience and tolerance to make one family work. Most of us have a somewhat egocentric orientation to the world. We tend to assume that our own way of doing things is unquestionably better than other ways. Because of this natural bias, we need to remind ourselves that other ways of behaving are just as valid as our own. Learning about Dominance Profiles is a good introduction to the thinking styles and behavior of other people. At the very least, this knowledge helps us to anticipate how others will respond under stress — thus increasing the potential for deeper understanding within relationships. Knowledge of one another's Dominance Profiles can help everyone in the family, classroom, or workplace to honor and appreciate one another more.

We tend to pick partners that have different learning styles and respond differently under stress than we do. We also tend to have children with different ways of processing. These differences help to enrich our lives, but they can also become the basis of misunderstandings and disharmony. Understanding our learning styles and those of our partners and children allows us to be more compassionate with one another and with ourselves. Facing our quirks and idiosyncrasies allows us to appreciate variety, and the different things we can learn from each other.

This appreciation for diverse, complementary ways of behaving is essential in the workplace too. In businesses, people who work together should understand how bosses and co-workers are likely to process, plan and create under the stress of business. Dominance Profiles also provide valuable information as to how people will best work together for the benefit of the business, given their particular strengths.

Dominance Profiles and Relationships

In the following pages I have collected some stories to help you see how Dominance Profiles influence our behavior in relationships. These are all true to life situations that illustrate stress-filled or new learning situations. In each case, I've attempted to show how the people involved react under stress given their basal profiles.

Driving with My Daughter

This first story is of a predicament that occurred when my daughter Breeze was learning to drive. She and I were both in the car, with Breeze at the wheel. Here are our profiles.

We had just finished having breakfast in a restaurant on our way to California. Driving with her learner's permit, Breeze backed out of the parking spot and was driving (*very slowly*) along a line of parked cars on the left. One of the manifestations of her blocked dominant foot (same side as dominant hemisphere) was that she drove very slowly when she was first learning to drive.

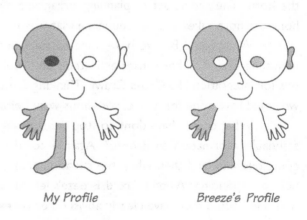

My Profile   Breeze's Profile

Being on the right side of the car with my right eye dominant, I naturally looked to the left and was able to see a big white Cadillac with two very old people backing out, and I knew they couldn't see us. Because Breeze is left eye dominant, she was looking to the right and didn't see the Cadillac. Being gestalt dominant, I immediately saw the whole picture and visualized them backing right into Breeze's door and hurting her. Because the image frightened me so badly, I couldn't speak in a logical way and started making all sorts of frantic sounds while pointing at the Cadillac.

Because Breeze is left eye and left ear dominant she had to turn her head toward me to get the information. Also because of her limited foot, she stopped the car *right behind the Cadillac that was still slowly backing out.* She kept asking me what was the matter, and all I could do was make survival sounds and point. Because she was now frightened, she could only look and listen to me — and not turn to see what was happening. Because of her gestalt dominance, she was missing the pieces (like my pointing) that would have let her know why I was acting so strangely.

Fortunately, the Cadillac stopped two inches from Breeze's door. I had nightmares about it for weeks to come. Breeze asked me why I had not just reached over and honked the horn. The simple act of planning, organizing my muscles to reach over and actually honk the horn takes a linear sequence that was totally inaccessible to me at the time.

What could Breeze have done to start out driving that morning with both her hemispheres and all her senses activated? She could have done some Brain Gym® activities for integration like Cross Crawls, Thinking Caps and Lazy 8's for the eyes or yoga, or we could have gone for a nice, conscious walk before driving.

What could I have done to stop the survival reaction, think clearly and give understandable information to Breeze? Again, I could have started out relaxed from a nice, conscious walk and then when the situation arose, taken a moment to sit in Hook Up's before responding. When relaxed, Breeze's left ear would accept the specifics of information, and I could then have clearly advised her on exactly what to do.

The trick is to take the time, a few seconds to a few minutes, to prepare the whole mind/body system for the next adventure. Russian families traditionally do this routinely. Whenever anyone is about to take a trip the whole family sits quietly for five minutes before leaving. It is a wonderful practice to quiet and integrate the mind.

A Tale of Two Piano Teachers

Again from my own experience, this story has to do with learning to play the piano from my *very* logic hemisphere dominant piano teacher. Here are our profiles:

My first teacher, when I was 7 years old, placed a strong emphasis on timing and note reading and he expected me to master these concepts right away. He even had my mother buy a metronome (which I hated). When I didn't get the notes or

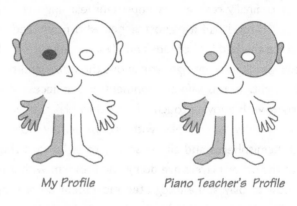

My Profile　　　Piano Teacher's Profile

timing right he would hit my hands with a baton which caused me to totally shut down all sensory input. Because his dominant hand was opposite his logic hemisphere, he needed to talk a lot during my lesson. To this day I can't remember a thing he said to me, but I do remember picking up the emotional frustration he was feeling. I'm sure he was as stressed as I was.

He presented the linear, logical pieces of musical notation and expected me to easily follow what to him seemed simple. Being a visual learner he would point to the note and say "can't you see that?" I had a hard time seeing or hearing anything after the first intimidating whack of the baton. I'm sure I also appeared stubborn because I never said anything except "yes," since I couldn't access my language hemisphere when stressed. Because of his blocked ear, he wouldn't have heard me, but he needed to talk to figure out why this was so difficult for me.

As a teenager, in a fit of frustration, I secretly buried the metronome in the back yard — one of the most liberating things I have ever done.

In spite of my teacher, I loved the piano when I was alone and could make up my own tunes, express my young girl emotions through it, and create my own rhythm to the music I had been assigned to practice. I needed to learn through image and emotion in order to finally realize how important learning the notes and timing were.

Later, I had a piano teacher who mothered me and whose home I loved to go to since she had lots of kids and always made bread. She would sit on my right side and speak gently into my right ear about the notes and timing and would pat my back when I did it right. In this safe environment, as she accessed my dominant ear and anchored the learning with a loving touch, I learned to play the piano.

Today, when I play with groups on my violin or piano, I need the integration of both hemispheres and all my senses to sight read the notes with the right timing, know what the other players are doing and perform with image and passion. When I was learning how to play, some integrated movement before my lessons would have assisted both my piano teacher and I. It would have helped him to be more aware of my specific learning style and work with me more effectively. And in a more integrated state, I would not have been so intimidated by him. Even now, integrated movements are beneficial to my playing.

Two Profiles, One Marriage

In marriage, we often pick people with very different profiles from our own. This arrangement has great advantages if each partner is willing to learn from and acknowledge the gifts of the other. However, under times of stress or new learning, the couple's styles of processing may be so different that there is very little common ground for understanding. This situation can also occur between a parent and child, between siblings, or between business partners. This was the case with my marriage to Breeze's father, Jim.

Jim and I taught Biology together at the Community College of Denver where we met. He was an excellent theoretical biologist and teacher, careful to acknowledge and work with the most current, exact research and findings to present to a class of students.

He was a good lecturer, mostly focusing on interesting details and sometimes bringing in the whole picture as he saw it with his dominant eye. He was also a good listener because of his dominant ear, and tended to seek out the details and specifics.

Jim's Profile   My Profile

Our teaching styles were quite different. He enjoyed lecturing and digging out the current specifics, while I preferred experiential teaching — taking my students on field trips, or into the laboratory where I emphasized discovery through hands-on lab experiments. My lectures were full of visual aids, "show and tell" graphics or biological specimens, and active discussion.

I was very spontaneous in my approach — if I wanted to learn something (like alternative energy or the useful plants of Colorado), I simply said I would teach the course the next semester. Because I was excited about the material, therefore integrated, I easily collected the visual and auditory details of information, prepared as best I could and gave my students projects on other aspects of the subject so that I became the student also. Jim would not teach a new course until he had thoroughly researched it and planned the whole curriculum, which usually took two to three years.

We learned much from each other — I, how to research, plan and present material in a sequential way; Jim, how to be more spontaneous and experiential in his presentations. We were a good match except when marital stress would pop up.

When Jim and I would get into an argument, he would start by asking me "What is the matter?" In my mind it wasn't just one thing that was "the matter." It was everything — I could see it only as a complete image usually with a lot of emotional injustice involved. As I would begin to explain in my verbally inhibited, emotional way my image of the "everything", he would find a book and go away to read.

At the time, I believed that he retreated to his books because he didn't love me, but it was because he was overwhelmed by the big picture I presented him. He couldn't find any pieces to start working out the problem. And because he was so out of touch with his emotions, mine frightened him.

If we did pursue the matter (which didn't often occur — notice our blocked feet), he would talk about all the specifics in a logical way and want me to understand. He would explain what I/we should do and then be upset if I didn't do it. In my frustration at his not understanding me, I couldn't hear or see his logic because my ears and eyes were blocked. I felt lots of emotion and couldn't communicate it with reasoned words, so I would end up crying, which just served to make me feel more inadequate. I'm sure he also felt inadequate at helping, and we would both miss each other totally.

We actually came up with a plan to help us communicate better. When I was upset, but still integrated enough to spell out the specific things bothering me, I would sit down and make a list. I would then hand the list to him which would give him a place to start. However, it was still difficult for him to access his emotions and understand mine, and the reasons I was upset. Instead he would just enumerate the things that he thought would "fix it."

If in our frustration we had taken a few moments to do some integrative movements, we might have been able to understand each other better. We both noticed that it helped if we walked together while working on conflicts. My daughter and I have found that if we do Lazy 8's together for my blocked eye, and then walk when we argue, that the emotional charge is dissipated and we are able to see and understand each other more clearly. As a counselor, I have used integrated movement to reduce friction after students have been fighting. I would have them sit in Hook Ups for two minutes and then do Lazy 8's with each other before discussing what happened. It helped immensely.

Matching Profiles Don't Necessarily Work Better Together

When you get two people together who have the same profiles, there can also be a problem in times of stress or new learning. Take for example the situation of two logic hemisphere people with limited eyes and ears interacting or coming up with a business plan. They will need to talk and analyze all the details of the project, but each may have difficulty hearing what the other is saying or seeing what the other is doing.

If the situation is relaxed, as in a fun brainstorming session, the ear and eye will be accessing their gestalt hemispheres, allowing them to hear and see the big picture and process the pieces into it. But if stress creeps in, their similar profiles will make it difficult for each to see or hear

A's Profile   B's Profile

the big picture that the other has been able to access, leaving them mired in the details. Because neither of their feet are blocked, they will plow through with the details anyway, doing lots of specific, piecemeal things, but having a hard time pulling it all together into a big picture, idea or plan.

If this is a business or company that must be innovative to survive (as most businesses are), they will need to be as integrated as possible to access the whole picture as well as the details. It is always advantageous to have different learning profiles available to enrich and broaden the scope and possibilities in a company and for all the players to create from a place of integration, rather than stress. Programs such as Brain Gym,® yoga, Qi Gong, or Tai Chi are highly effective in breaking the stress cycle, so that full potential is accessed. In Japan, many businessmen and women start their day with Tai Chi and are more productive because of it.

Two Ways to Paint Fish

My good friend Cherokee is a wonderful artist who loves to paint the reef fish she encounters whenever she swims or dives in Hawaii. I also love to paint and draw, but don't consider myself much of an artist though many of my paintings have made their way into friends' and family homes as gifts. Our profiles help explain why our approaches to art are so strikingly different.

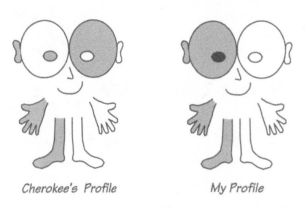

Cherokee's Profile   My Profile

Cherokee's preferred way of doing art from her profile is to scuba dive and really study the fish, noting their size, shape, habitat and especially their colors. She then goes to the library for more information and pictures of the fish. Then, using her calipers for exact measurements she is able to plan the picture and draw it. Once drawn to her satisfaction, she matches the paint colors to paint the most perfect life-like fish, fresh from the sea. She uses her eyes and ears to pick up the specifics and then is able to transcribe those through her art. Cherokee also teaches art to her students in a highly creative and flexible way, letting them each find their medium and approach to doing art. An excellent, integrated teacher, she honors the artistic style of others.

On the other hand, when I do art from my preferential profile I may find a place in the woods with my pencil and paper away from any distractions. When the spirit moves me, I sketch freehand whatever interests me, which is usually twisted trees with faces in their gnarled structure. If I choose to paint, I prefer to pick whichever color feels right to me at the time and just paint freeform until another color is called for. I enjoy watching what shapes emerge and how the colors work or don't work together. By using my dominant observer eye, accessing my logic hemisphere, I am able to draw or paint realistically, but I must first be emotionally inspired.

Both Cherokee and I find that integrative movement assists our art, and every other part of our lives. When I get stuck and know I must do a drawing (as for this book), I will take a long walk, consciously accessing all my senses. True art (creativity) comes from being able to access the pieces as well as the whole.

The Eighth Grade Algebra Dilemma

This is a real situation that occurred at an Intermediate school where I was a counselor for children who were having problems in school. It had to do with an eighth grade algebra student and her teacher. Here are their profiles:

This student was sent to me because she was failing algebra. After assessing her Dominance Profile, I was surprised that she was having any difficulty. With her logic hemisphere dominant, she should have been able to pick up the linear sequencing necessary to understand algebra. And with her dominant right ear going into her logic hemisphere,

Student's Profile

Teacher's Profile

she should have had no problem with remembering the formulas or details of algebra.

When I asked how she was doing in her other courses, she said she was doing A or B work. I was not surprised because she had a good profile for the normal school curriculum, except for her eye, but most eighth grade courses were lecture based and didn't require initial visual input.

I decided to sit in on her algebra class to see if I could get a clue as to why she was having problems. The teacher had put her in the front of the class, right in front of him. When he talked about an algebra problem or wrote it on the board, the girl would close her eyes and turn her right ear toward him. He would look at her in disgust and say "Look at me. Look at the board!" As soon as she had to look at him with her limited eye, she would lose the whole concept.

We all learned something that day. Because the teacher was such a visual learner, he expected his students to also be visual learners and always look at him. This is typical in many classrooms where teachers insist on "Eyes forward," or believe that the students are learning only if they are looking at the teacher or the board. People like this student, who are auditory learners with limited eyes under stress, may need to close their eyes or look elsewhere when attempting to understand a difficult concept.

The teacher took immediate action (stepping forward with his dominant foot), apologizing to the student and asking her where she would prefer to sit. She chose a seat two rows back on the left side of the room where she could fully access with her dominant right ear and not bother him if she didn't look at him. She began doing integrated movements to more fully access her eye and within weeks, her algebra grades had improved greatly.

Dominance Profiles give us useful tools to assist others, learn to understand our mistakes and be more fully present with other people. Through this process, the teacher also began working on his limited hearing under stress so that he could better listen to his students when they had difficulties. He admitted that when students came to him with problems, like the student who was failing, he would tell them to simply watch what he was doing. In this case, she needed him to verbalize the process in a logical manner instead. In cases with very kinesthetic students, he could have been more helpful by having them work with math manipulatives or do the math problem while he watched. Knowing about Dominance Profiles helped him to greatly broaden his teaching skills and become a highly effective teacher.

Knowing the dominance pattern of another person, you don't have to waste time trying to get through to them, feeling frustrated or irritated. And by knowing your own profile, you can honor those tendencies in yourself, maximizing your life.

Now — using your own profile, think of people in your life and your interactions with them. Notice how your Dominance Profile can affect your first reactions under stress and how you prefer to learn. Also be aware of how you have learned to compensate in social situations with other people. Our uniqueness is very important because it gives the world another way to look at and do things. I have only presented a small piece of what affects our lives — how we see, hear, process and communicate things. There are many other factors, so I invite you to explore. You will probably find, as I have, that people are most interesting subjects with lots of gifts to offer, to learn and grow from. ENJOY!

☀ 6 ☀

Dominance Profiles and Education

In 1990 I undertook a formal study to compare students' Dominance Profiles with the systems the schools were using to classify learners. For instance, I wanted to see if there were correlations between labels like "Gifted and Talented" and particular Dominance Profiles. In fact, I did find that overall, people with logic hemisphere dominant profiles were heavily represented in the Gifted and Talented category, whereas students with gestalt or sensory limited profiles were heavily represented in Special Education groups.

Having used the Dominance Profiles for more than twenty years with thousands of individuals, I've found that, unfortunately, my initial study from 1990 still holds true for school children. I have found that it is not only true in the U.S., but in other countries as well. So, I have decided to include the results of my study in this book in order to illustrate the need for Dominance Profile assessment in schools and to share what I see as short-comings of the education labels currently being used.

In 1990 using the basal Dominance Profiles, I collected data from a random sample of 218 students attending schools in Denver, Colorado and Kona, Hawaii. These students were identified by the following labels according to assessment criteria used in these schools:

Gifted & Talented: Children chosen for this program excelled academically and had high SAT scores, thus succeeded at language and math skills.

Normal: Children doing OK in the regular classroom.

Remedial: Children who are struggling with reading.

Special Education/Emotionally Handicapped: Children labeled with specific learning difficulties such as Attention Deficit Hyperactive Disorder (ADHD), Aspergers or Dyslexia.

High School Redirection: An alternative high school for students who had previously dropped out of or been suspended from their high schools

The following graph shows my findings with percentages of each group checked. (The columns representing logic and gestalt for each group total 100%.)

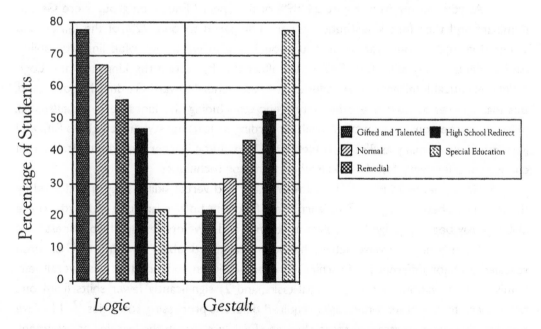

Figure 24: Hemisphere Dominance in a Random Sample of 218 Students Attending Denver and Kona, Hawaii High Schools

According to this study, students labeled Gifted and Talented and Normal were predominantly logic hemisphere dominant, whereas the Special Education students were mostly gestalt dominant learners.

Logic hemisphere dominant students tend to demonstrate high linear and verbal abiliites. In school, they are more often positively reinforced with the Gifted and Talented label. They are more likely to have high self-esteem and experience less stress because schoolwork and testing is geared toward their competencies. This allows them the confidence to explore gestalt avenues of learning. (But only if they are not overly stressed by competition and the pursuit of ever higher grades.) With less stress in the long run, they have a better chance of obtaining more integrative learning strategies.

As you can see from Figure 24, 89% of the Special Education group were Gestalt dominant and therefore kinesthetic learners, compared to only 22% of the Gifted and Talented group. In our traditional educational system we highly value linguistic ability. And students sitting still. Our SAT tests reflect this by testing the Linguistic and Logical/Mathematical Intelligences. As educational researcher Howard Gardner has observed, this bias ignores at least five other intelligences, including the kinesthetic, visual/spatial, musical, interpersonal and intrapersonal. According to learning style researchers Rita and Kenneth Dunn as many as 85% of students are kinesthetic learners, yet the typical school curriculum offers very few if any kinesthetic learning techniques.

Gestalt learners tend to have lower linear and verbal skills. They are affected by the early push, between ages 5-7, to learn linear functions both in language and math. These children may begin to judge themselves as "dumb" and develop "learned helplessness."

A study of brain wave activity between "learning disabled" and "normal" children revealed a major difference. "Learning disabled" children, exhibited 1) less overall left-hemisphere activation, even with verbal tasks, and 2) significantly fewer shifts from one hemisphere to the other when tasks required different processing strategies.[27] I believe this directly relates to stress in these children. Due to stress in the learning environment, they end up depending only on their dominant hemisphere (gestalt). They become unable to explore and adequately access their logic hemisphere. When overly stressed they might become overwhelmed with the big picture, unable to see the details or communicate with others. Thus they are trapped in a vicious cycle. The stress of schooling heightens their inability to learn in a logical way and discourages communication between both hemispheres. Discrimination against Gestalt learners has been very strong in our society.

Gestalt learners have to struggle to make it through our educational system. I believe Albert Einstein was a gestalt learner. His early academic career suggests this. He eventually graduated from Federal Polytechnic University in Switzerland, but without any particular acclaim. Fortunately, he sought out holistic learning situations that fed his curiosity and lust for understanding. And the world has been the beneficiary of his incredible insights; all of which were more intimately bound to his internal images and feelings than to strictly linear processing.[28]

Our educational system does little to encourage holistic, intuitive, image-based (as opposed to verbal-based) thinking. But where would we be without these capacities? Gestalt learners have talents that are too frequently undervalued in school. If, as a result, gestalt learners undervalue themselves we run the risk that they stop contributing in significant ways. We must strive to understand and facilitate the learning process of gestalt learners so we do not lose this valuable resource.

Sensory Access

Our educational system favors students who process linearly, take in information auditorially, look at the teacher when they are talking (visual) and can repeat the pieces of information back in a logical, linear fashion. These are students with the full sensory access Profile A. Yet, they made up, on average, only 15% of the test population. The Gifted and Talented group had the largest number of full sensory access learners, while the Special Ed group had the largest number of full sensory limited learners. (See Figure 25.)

These full sensory access learners usually do well on the verbal and mathematical skills tests commonly given in our schools, including the Scholastic Achievement Tests

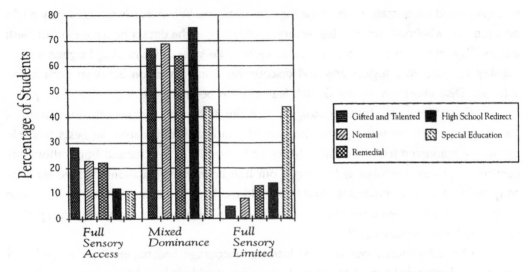

Figure 25: Sensory Access Patterns in the Same 218 Students

(SAT's) which despite their limited scope, are considered in the United States to be reliable assessments of intelligence. You will notice that this profile is highly dependent on logic hemisphere functioning. But if these learners are not encouraged to use gestalt hemisphere processing they may not adequately develop such very important abilities as relating emotionally with other people, seeing the big picture, feeling the emotional implications of ideas, or spontaneously generating new ideas.

Dominant Ear

In my study, the auditory limited profile represents an average of approximately 52% of the population (see Figure 26). Yet lecturing is our primary way of teaching. A typical lecture, then, is likely to be missed by over half of the audience.

Also notice that a high percentage of both the Gifted and Talented and the Special Education students were auditory limited. This discrepancy in labeling can be explained

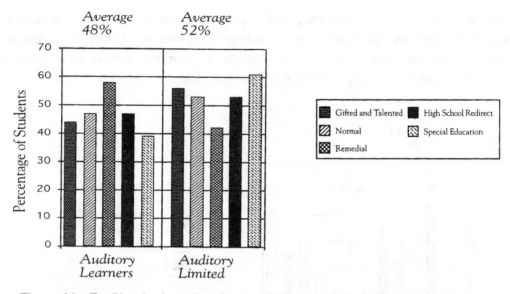

Average 48%   **Average 52%**

Percentage of Students

Legend:
- Gifted and Talented
- Normal
- Remedial
- High School Redirect
- Special Education

Auditory Learners   Auditory Limited

Figure 26: Ear/Hemisphere Dominance Patterns in the Same 218 Students

when you consider that the vast majority of Gifted and Talented students are logic dominant and therefore verbal. So, even though they are auditory limited and may not hear what is being said, they talk — and so are believed to be more intelligent. The opposite is true for Special Education students, mainly gestalt dominant, who are not verbal when stressed, and are therefore considered to be 'dumb' (not speaking/not intelligent).

Dominant Eye

We also tend to believe that people are listening only if they are looking at us when we are speaking. Being a teacher for so long, I know it does feel good to have people looking at me when I talk, but notice in Figure 27 the columns marked visual limited. This represents any profile where the dominant eye is on the same side as the dominant hemisphere. With only 27.8% of the GT group compared to 72.2% of the Special Education group being visually limited, there might be an overemphasis on visual learning in the classroom. Again, approximately 50% of people are visually limited. If concepts are new and difficult to understand, and/or emotionally volatile, visually limited persons may need to look away (out the window, for example), or shut their eyes in order to take in the information more easily through their dominant senses. Unfortunately, this is often construed as inattentiveness.

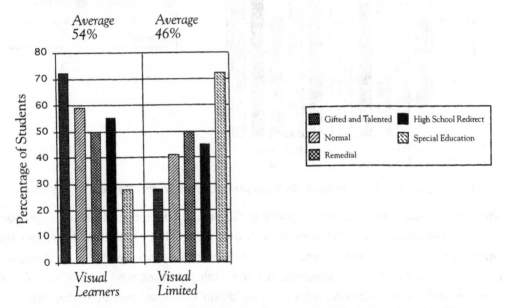

Figure 27: Eye/Hemisphere Dominance Patterns in the Same 218 Students

The visually limited profile also affects ease of reading, especially in stressful circumstances. Under stress, the eyes will react by moving peripherally to see where the danger lies. During stress, if asked to read, the dominant eye will continue to check for danger and the non-dominant eye will be left to read. This greatly decreases comprehension. You may have noticed that when you are stressed, you have to reread things over and over to finally understand what is being said.

Left eye dominance has another consequence for learners. We are not truly binocular. That large protuberance between your eyes — your nose, interferes with complete binocular vision. So, we have one main tracking eye, the dominant eye. The other eye follows. The right eye naturally tracks from left to right while the left eye naturally tracks from right to left.

A person with a left eye dominant pattern will want to look at the right side of the

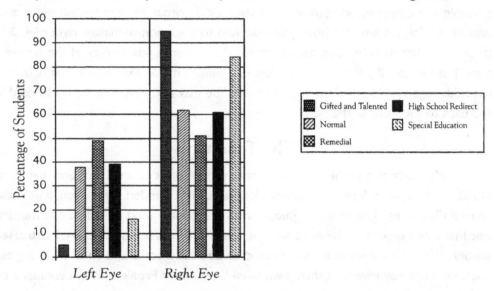

Figure 28: Eye Dominance in the Same 218 Students

page first and then move to the left. In languages that are read from right to left (Hebrew or Chinese) left eyed students would have the edge. Perhaps they would be the Gifted and Talented students, reading easily and therefore gaining acclaim.

Notice that in my study, the "remedial" students have a higher percentage of left eye dominance (see Figure 28). Eighty-one percent of these students are left eyed/right handed. Since the left eye naturally wants to track from the right to the left, it will also guide the hand from the right to the left which may cause writing difficulties or letter reversals. These are the children in Chapter I (Title I) programs that reverse letters and numbers and have difficulty with beginning reading. When the eyes are stress-free and integrated, they can track together in the opposite direction, making reading English easier.

If you have a basal profile that indicates left eye dominance using the muscle checking, yet you came up with a right eye dominance on the self-assessment, this is an example of a compensation (adaptation) strategy. In order to read English more easily, a crucial skill for success in school, you switched to your non-dominant right eye, since it tracks from left to right. This demonstrates the immense adaptability of the human system. Just for fun: if you are basically left eye dominant, you may notice that it is easy to read this page upside down from right to left. You may also have a tendency to read from the back to the front of the book or magazine.

The Teachers

My study also profiled the teachers in the subject schools. Seventy-five percent (75%) of them were logic hemisphere dominant, right handed, right eyed, and auditory limited (Profile B). Under stress people with this profile tend to talk about the details, not listen, and expect students to look at them. Of course teachers are as stressed as anyone else, maybe even more so. With crowded classrooms and children acting out in class, teachers may revert to their own basal Dominance Profiles. Stress creates a circle of frustration for everyone concerned.

Full Sensory Limited Learners

People that are full sensory limited have difficulty taking in sensory information, moving or speaking when under stress. They will shut down, withdraw, and process internally using their preferential hemisphere (just the details for the Logic dominant, and just the images and emotions for the Gestalt dominant people). Figure 25 presents a comparative graphing of this group in the columns marked full sensory limited. Only 5% of the

Gifted and Talented students are fully limited, compared to 44% of the Special Education group. The most disadvantaged group of learners in our traditional school system are those who are Gestalt dominant full sensory limited, (Profiles L and LL).

It is important for persons with Profiles L and LL to have quiet time alone to process stressful situations. Again, in our very verbal society, we want people to articulate their thoughts and feelings. Gestalt fully limited learners may see the big picture, but have difficulty expressing it in language. In their frustration at not being able to verbalize, they may strike out emotionally. They may end up in fights or become emotionally volatile in the classroom, home or workplace, thus earning the label of emotionally handicapped. Or the stress may be so great that they must move, so they fidget and wiggle, ending up with labels like: ADD or ADHD.

Gestalt fully limited people can be assisted when several factors are included in the learning environment. These include: 1) using integrated movements to learn, 2) getting the whole picture first, then tying in the details later, 3) starting linear processing like printing, reading, spelling, linear math functions at age seven to eight, not before, 4) feeling secure in their emotions and relationships, and 5) taking quiet time out to process new learning in an intrapersonal way. With highly traditional crowded classrooms, mostly logic hemisphere dominant teachers, and curricula based on detail first, these limited learners spend a lot of time in survival mode. This can lead to "learned helplessness" and the astoundingly large numbers of gestalt learners in our expensive Special Education and Emotionally Handicapped programs.

As I worked with the wonderful children in the Special Education and Emotionally Handicapped programs at various schools, I could see through their frustration to the unheralded intelligence inside each of them. Interestingly, when they are integrated, using both hemispheres, they can easily take in the visual and auditory details (it is actually their preference), are able to place the details into a global context and verbally share this information in an understandable way with others. They can even follow detailed directions. I've found them to be spontaneous and to excel in kinesthetic, musical, visual/

spatial and interpersonal ways. This also applies to the Logic fully limited profile. When they are integrated, using both hemispheres, they can visually and preferentially take in the big picture, auditorily listen for the story/metaphor/emotion and place these in a logical context to explain to others. They can also spontaneously move to music with rhythm and confidence. By honoring the arts, integrated movement and interpersonal relationships more in our schools and society, these people can share their special gifts and become important assets to our world.

Gestalt Hemisphere Problem Solving

Though our educational system espouses and rewards logic hemisphere problem solving, the role of the gestalt hemisphere in problem solving is gaining recognition. One researcher, Grayson Wheatley, has addressed an aspect of right hemisphere problem solving which I recognize as my own specific way of processing math, particularly algebra.

According to Wheatley[29], the right hemisphere excels in tasks that are non-verbal, spatial and less familiar. It grasps the whole and solves the problems at once. The left hemisphere processes the stimulus information so the stimulus can be described in language. In problem solving, it is important not to force children to use language as the vehicle for thought when imaging is more appropriate. Children can know without being able to state their thoughts in words. Bob Samples elaborates this thinking by noting that problem solving requires restructuring of elements, not just following rules.[30]

We are still leaning too heavily on algorithmic (linear, mathematical, rule-oriented) learning, still expecting students to learn primarily through rote memorization, all the way up through college. Why? Memory and linear skills are easy to test and quantify. That's why! These kinds of tests give objective comparisons. But what do they measure? Facts and linear skills are useful acquisitions, but are they the most important part of a person's education? Shouldn't we be more concerned about thinking, creativity, application of knowledge to real life situations. The emphasis on low-level skills and memory testing fosters an emphasis on low-level thought processing — teaching to tests. Consequently, practice in high level thinking can be and often is shortchanged. As Herman Epstein has observed, "More than half the population in the United States never reach the Piaget stage of formal reasoning. We have knowers but few thinkers!"[31]

The stress of constant testing diminishes the ability to see problem solving in a larger context. It turns education into a numbers game where competition, rather than cooperation, is encouraged and information is not moved to applicability or creative thought. If we can advance to an education that balances memory and thinking, and honors each person's learning style, agile learners with valuable thinking tools can emerge. Or to put it more cerebrally, as Bob Samples does: "We discovered that if the right hemisphere functions are celebrated, the development of left hemisphere qualities becomes inevitable."

Brain Plasticity

Research is showing that our brains are very plastic. We are able to compensate and actually change our dominance pattern to fit different situations in our life. As we grow, we learn what actions or ideas will make it easier for us to accommodate different situations, and rather than becoming fully integrated, we lean on these compensations to "get us through." When obtaining a present moment compensation profile using muscle checking, it may be different from the basal profile and is often unilateral if the person is under stress. These compensations may provide us with a survival tactic at the moment, but in the long run limit our ability to experience our full potential on a regular basis. I have found that when people do simple cross-lateral integrated movements like those found in Brain Gym®, yoga, Tai Chi, Qi Gong and physical interpersonal play, their profiles will be fully integrated, accessing both hemispheres and all the senses. They can then readily take in the environment and learn. Releasing stress and having both hemispheres fully available on a regular basis is the key to a successful, passionate, life full of curiosity, new learning, deeply satisfying relationships and optimal creativity.

Teaching to the Whole Brain

Sandra Zachary, a third grade teacher in Hawaii, had her students figure out their own basal Dominance Profiles at the beginning of the school year, using the muscle checking assessment. She then had them organize themselves according to their easiest sensory access: visual learners in front; auditory learners in the next row with right ear dominants on the left side of the room and left ear dominants on the right side of the room; and the gestalt fully limited in the back of the room with clay or wax to manipulate kinesthetically during class.

For her class, it became a strong lesson in self-understanding and compassion for others. Labels like "Stupid" or "Nerd" were dropped as students became aware of the learning preferences of their peers, and how and why they would respond when stressed. Each student taped their Dominance Profile to their desk so other students could see it and relate to them with understanding. Sandra would hear students say: "Michael is upset right now and needs to be left alone because he has the Einstein profile," or, "Tell Claudia how you feel into her left ear, the other doesn't work well when she is sad."

Each day — at the beginning of the day, after recess and after lunch — the whole class did Brain Gym® activities for five minutes. At the end of six weeks, students were allowed to change seats, which they did with a deeper understanding of their preferential patterns and learning strengths. The stress levels in the classroom had become minimal and classroom management had become a cooperative process for everyone. In the end, each student gained the highest academic success they had yet achieved in their schooling.

To honor each student's learning style, consciously add stories to the details presented, every ten to fifteen minutes have learners tell someone else what they have learned in order to anchor the information in memory, use visuals, dramatics and imaginative play with ideas (brainstorming), and sprinkle integrative movement throughout the learning situation.

The health of our educational system depends on our nurturing and promoting the learning of all our citizens. We must relinquish judgments that lead to stress-provoking labels and competition. An appropriate thinking curriculum must be established that synthesizes whole mind/body processing through regular art, music and movement in conjunction with cognitive skills. We must give learners mind/body integrative tools such as Brain Gym® and others suggested in Appendix B which allow them to stop the stress cycle and activate full sensory/hemisphere access. Perhaps then we can fully realize the unique human potential that Paul MacLean invokes, in an evolving society where all people succeed at learning, for a lifetime.

Appendices:

How Muscle Checking Works

Learning Aids and Strategies

Sources for Further Information

Notes

Index

Appendix A

How Muscle Checking Works

Muscle testing (checking) as an indicator for bodily function and information was developed by Dr. George Goodheart in 1964. [32, 33] His discovery came from the work of Terence Bennett (chiropractor, 1920's), Frank Chapman (osteopath, 1930's), R. W. Lovett (orthopedic surgeon, 1932) and Drs. Henry and Florence Kendall (work with polio patients, 1949).[34] With the proper intention and procedure, it is a very accurate way to assess the body's hardwired conscious and subconscious beliefs and structural functions such as the basal dominance pattern.[35, 36, 37, 38, 39]

Our current physiological understanding of the intricate structure of muscle fibers reveals a feedforward/feedback system via spindle fibers and golgi tendon bodies, which acts as a monitoring gauge on the fibers. Each muscle in the body has thousands of muscle fibers. At any one time, some of the muscle fibers are relaxed, while other muscle fibers are contracted. This is called "muscle tonus." This feedback keeps the muscles from being overused or injured.

The brain is constantly monitoring each muscle fiber and tendon through information coming from the spindle apparatus (primary and secondary afferent axons), or the golgi tendon bodies. This information goes to the sensory cortex of the neo-cortex, letting the brain know the tension on each muscle and where it is in space (called proprioception). The brain can then decide how it wants to change the muscle to do a certain task, usually subconsciously. Information is sent via the gamma and beta efferent nerve fibers to the nuclear bag and chain fibers stimulating the muscle fiber to either contract or relax to accomplish the task.

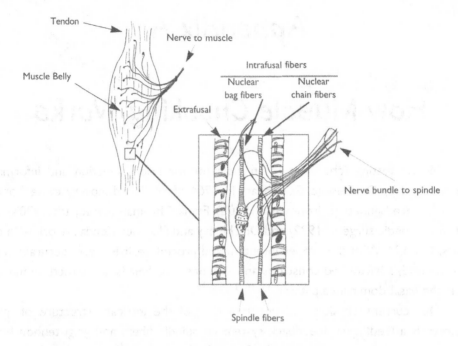

Figure 29: *Spindle Fibers in Muscle*

In simple words, the spindle fibers and golgi tendon bodies within the muscle and tendon are acting like a gauge giving feedback to the brain and readjusting the gauge in line with the brain's intention.

We can tap into the body's information system through this intricate feedforward/ feedback system by setting a specific intention and then muscle checking. With muscle checking, the muscle becomes a transducer for the subconscious or innate patterns that are difficult to access directly. The intention becomes the key factor to input into the spindle fiber, adjusting its sensitivity, like a gauge or meter. The facilitator and subject determine the setting of the gauge with their intention to find the basal dominance pattern (profile) of this specific person. Perot, Meldener, and Gouble found that the intention needed to be the same between the examiner and subject on order to be reliable.[40]

The intention to obtain an accurate basal Dominance Profile accesses what has been programmed into the person beginning at around nine weeks of age in utero, as the dominant, most stable or key lead function during stress or new learning. With basal profiles, we are looking for a locked muscle when we bring attention to a specific eye, ear, hand, foot and hemisphere of the brain. If what we are checking is dominant, it is our intention that the muscle easily "locks" the shoulder joint against the challenge to the muscle (pushing down with 2 pounds of pressure for 2 seconds). If what we are checking is not dominant, our intention is that the muscle will not lock, but release in response.

The muscle checking procedure is easy to learn, but takes practice to perfect. It has been an important tool for me, not only in my work, but also in becoming more sensitive and aware of my body's subconscious and innate messages. A very validating experience in muscle checking occurred for me with a group of Occupational Therapists in South Africa. These professionals were highly trained, had private practices, and had also taught in the Medical Department at the University for many years. Muscle checking confirmed all of the dominance assessments they had already made with the children they were working with. It also gave solid information, especially about hand dominance, that they had a difficult time assessing using their previous professional training. They were so impressed with its accuracy, they began using the muscle checking exclusively, saving themselves and their clients hours of testing and assessment work.

Appendix B

Learning Aids and Strategies

Active Listening

The practice of bringing full attention to the act of listening in order to take in as much of the information, motive, and context from spoken words. Following are some good sources for further information on improving your listening skills.

Mortimer J. Adler suggests that good listening is similar to good reading. He offers a guide to listening in his book, **How To Speak, How to Listen**, Macmillan, New York, 1983.

A simple and effective two person listening exercise called *The Think & Listen* is described by Peter Kline in his book, **The Everyday Genius**, Great River Books, Salt Lake City, 1988.

For more extensive training in listening skills see: Madelyn Burley-Allen's, **Listening, The Forgotten Skill**, John Wiley & Sons, New York, 1995. For improving listening skills in the workplace see: Warren H. Reed's **Positive Listening: Learning To Hear What People Are Really Saying**, Franklin Watts, New York, 1985 or Kevin J. Murphy's **Effective Listening: Hearing What People Say and Making It Work For You**, Bantam Books, New York, 1987.

Brain Gym®

Brain Gym is a set of simple and enjoyable cross-lateral integrated movements, brought together from many modalities by Dr. Paul Dennison and Gail Dennison from their work with Edu-Kinesthetics. The Brain Gym activities encourage whole brain Integration for all areas of learning throughout life by enabling learners to access parts of the brain previously unavailable to them. The changes in learning and behavior are often immediate and profound. Brain Gym is a registered trademark of the Educational Kinesiology Foundation. For information about Brain Gym and the Brain Gym activities contact Brain Gym International at: 1575 Spinnaker Drive, Suite 204B, Ventura, California 93001, phone: (800) 356-2109, *info@braingym.org.*

Brain Gym Activities

Brain Buttons — *activate points on the chest below the collar bone that increase oxygen to the brain and stimulate the vestibular system to wake up the brain*

Cross Crawls — *a cross-lateral standing crawl that activates integrated right and left hemisphere function*

Double Doodles — *an activity using both hands simultaneously making a mirror drawing that activates integrated right and left hemisphere function*

Elephants — *activates all areas of the mind/body system in a balanced way, especially the vestibular system*

Energy Yawn — *facilitates full nerve function across the temporal-mandibular joint and activates the vestibular system*

Hook Ups — *a calming activity that facilitates whole brain function to quiet and refocus yourself*

Lazy 8's — *a cross-lateral, midline movement using hand and eye coordination to improve integrated eye function and written communication*

The Owl — *relieves tension in the neck and shoulders, allowing more integrated hearing*

Thinking Caps — *stimulates the ears for active listening*

Vision Gym — *an extensive group of activities that facilitate optimal, integrated functioning of the eyes*

These activities are explained in detail in my book **Smart Moves, Why Learning Is Not All In Your Head**, Great River Books, Salt Lake City, 2nd Edition 2005 (*www.greatriverbooks.com*), which also explores the neurophysiological basis of Brain Gym and the impact of movement and physical activity on learning; also in the DVD **Education in Motion**, available through *heartconnect44@aol.com*. **Brain Gym,®** **Teachers Edition**, by Paul E and Gail E Dennison, Hearts at Play, Inc, a division of Edu-Kinesthetics, Inc., P.O. Box 3395, Ventura, Ca. 93006-3395. (800)356-2109.

Brainstorming

Brainstorming is a commonly used technique to loosen up thinking in groups of people working together, but which can also be used by individuals. The term was coined in the 1950's by Alex Osborne, an industrialist who encouraged brainstorming sessions among his managers to produce more innovation in the company. When brainstorming, the practice is to freely generate and spout out ideas in a playful way, without censoring any thoughts — wild, outrageous or otherwise. Further information about brainstorming and other creativity boosting practices can be found in **The Way of the Innovation Master** by Jerry Baumgartner, JPB Publishers, 2010 (*www.jpb.com*), **The Care and Framing of Strategic Innovation Challenges** by Arthur B. Vangundy (*avangundy@cox.net*), and Tom Wujec's **Five Star Mind, Games and Exercises to Stimulate Your Creativity and Imagination**, Doubleday, New York, 1995. Other brainstorming techniques can be found in Tony Buzan's **The Mind Map Book, How to Use Radiant Thinking to Maximize Your Brain's Untapped Potential**, Dutton, New York, 1994.

Creative Visualization

Creative visualization is another good way to generate ideas and boost your creativity. In a relaxed but alert mental state, freely associate and watch your internal, imagined thoughts in your mind's eye. Some helpful books are:

Shakti Gawain's **Creative Visualization**, New World Library, 2002. Marilee Zdenek's **The Right-Brain Experience, An Intimate Program to Free The Powers** *of Your Imagination*, McGraw Hill, New York, 1983; and Willis Harman and Howard Rheingold's *Higher Creativity, Liberating the Unconscious for Breakthrough Insights*, Jeremy Tarcher, Los Angeles, 1984. See also Susan Nolen-Hoeksena, et *al.*, *Rethinking Rumination*, in *Perspectives on Psychological Science*, Vol. 3 (5), 2008, p.400-424,

Flow Charts

A mapping method to break down the parts of a process so that the linear sequence of events and feedback loops in the process can be graphically represented. Flow charting is often used in computer programming but a good description of flow charting for generalized purposes can be found in Peter Kline and Laurence Martel's *School Success, The Inside Story*, Great River Books, Salt Lake City, 1992. See also, *Mind Tools – the eBook*, (*www.mindtools.com/pages/article/newTMC-97.htm*).

Magic Eye Books

A series of books that challenge your eyes to see hidden three dimensional pictures on a page printed with a two dimensional pattern. *Magic Eye Gallery: A Showing of 88 Images*, Andrews and McMeel, Kansas City, 1995; and, N. E. Thing, *Magic Eye: A New Way of Looking at the World*, Andrews and McMeel, Kansas City, 1993

Mind Maps

A way of graphically representing information in words and pictures with associated links between ideas. It was first developed by Tony Buzan in the 1970s as a memory aid, but has since been espoused as a useful tool to generate and organize ideas. Further information about mind mapping can be found in Tony Buzan's *The Mind Map Book, How to Use Radiant Thinking to Maximize Your Brain's Untapped Potential*, Dutton, New York, 1994. Also see Nancy Margulies *Mapping Inner Space, Learning and Teaching Mind Mapping*, Zephyr Press, Tucson, AZ, 1991; and *www.ThinkBuzan.com, www. mindmapping.com; www.smartdraw.com; www.mindtools.com/pages/article/newISS-01.htm*.

Mnemonics

There are many different techniques to boost your memory for anything from faces to formulas. Mnemonics help because they are based on the brain's own tendencies in memory processing. For many good memory techniques see: Joan Minninger's **Total Recall, How To Boost Your Memory Powers**, Rodale Press, Emmaus, PA, 1984, also, Peter Kline and Laurence Martel, **School Success, The Inside Story**, Great River Books, Salt Lake City, 1992; Eric Jensen, **Student Success Secrets**, Barron's Educational Series, New York, 1989, and Chris Brewer, **Soundtracks for Learning**, LifeSounds Educational Services, Bellingham, WA, 2008. See also *www.fun-with-words.com/mnemonics.html*, and *www.eudesign.com/mnems/*.

Outlining

A condensed list of the concepts in spoken or written text that identifies the main ideas and supporting details in a hierarchical, sequential order. Outlining is useful as a sequential, compact representation of ideas. However, if you are hoping to spur creative thinking and idea generation, mind mapping is a more powerful technique. Most books on study skills will contain instructions on how to outline topics. **School Success** by Peter Kline and Laurence Martel, Great River Books, Salt Lake City, 1992, is a good all around study skills workbook that teaches both left brain and right brain strategies for maximizing learning.

Prioritizing

Prioritizing organizes your activities by their overall importance to your goals and life. For good examples of prioritizing activities see Peter Kline and Laurence Martel, **School Success, The Inside Story**, Great River Books, Salt Lake City, 1992.

Time Management

Aids that help you get more things done in a day and achieve goals faster. Many books about study skills include tips and techniques to help you manage your time better. See Rita Phipps, **The Successful Student's Handbook**, University of Washington Press, Seattle, 1983, also, Julie Hahn's **Have You Done Your Homework? A Parent's Guide to Helping Teenagers Succeed in School**, John Wiley & Sons, New York, 1985. Also see various books on time management such as Ken Blanchard, **The One Minute Manager**, Morrow, New York, 1982.

Toning the Vowels

For developing sensitivity to sounds, especially for children who can't distinguish fast sound components in speech. Tone the vowels (A, E, I, O, U) by taking in a deep breath and saying the vowel in a long sustained manner as you breathe out. More benefit is gained if you use the whole mouth, full breath, and relax so the sound comes out more as a tone that vibrates. See Chris Brewer, **Soundtracks for Learning: Using Music in the Classroom,** LifeSounds Educational Services, Bellingham, WA, 2008

Sources for Further Information

Amen, Daniel G. *Magnificent Mind at Any Age: Natural Ways to Unleash Your Brain's Maximum Potential.* NY: Harmony Books, 2008.

Ayers, Jean. *Sensory Integration and Learning Disorders.* Los Angeles: Western Psychological Services, 1972.

Ayers, Jean. *Sensory Integration and the Child: 25th Anniversary Edition.* Los Angeles: Western Psychological Services, 2005.

Benzwie, Teresa. *A Moving Experience.* Tucson: Zephyr Press, 1987.

Benzwie, Teresa. *More Moving Experiences.* Tucson: Zephyr Press, 1996.

Bergeson, Eliza. *The YES! In SUCCESS, How to be the star you are and live the life you love.* Cornish Flat, NH: Singing Brook Press, 2011.

Brewer, Chris. *Soundtracks for Learning.* Bellingham, WA: LifeSounds Educational Services, 2008.

Brewer, Chris & Don Campbell. *Rhythms of Learning, Creative Tools for Developing Lifelong Skills.* Tucson: Zephyr Press, 1991.

Cohen, Bonnie Bainbridge. *Sensing, Feeling, and Action: The Experiential Anatomy of Body-Mind Centering.* Northampton, MA: Contact Editions, 2008.

Cohen, Isabel and Marcelle Goldsmith. *Hands On: How to Use Brain Gym® in the Classroom.* Ventura, CA: Edu-Kinesthetics, Inc., 2002.

Dennison, Gail E and Paul E. Dennison. *Visioncircles.* Ventura, CA: Edu-Kinesthetics, Inc., 1993.

Dennison, Paul E. and Gail E. *Personalized Whole Brain Integration.* Ventura, CA: Edu-Kinesthetics, Inc., 1985.

Dennison, Paul E. and Gail E. Dennison. *Brain Gym, Teachers Edition*, Revised. Ventura, CA: Edu-Kinesthetics, Inc., 2010.

Doidge, Norman. *The Brain That Changes Itself, Stories of Personal Triumph from the Frontiers of Brain Science*. NY: Penguin Books, 2007.

Dunn, Ken and Rita Dunn. *Teaching Young Children Through Their Individual Learning Styles*. N.Y.: Allyn & Bacon, 1992.

Education For Life Foundation. *Education For Life*. Education For Life Foundation, 14618 Tyler Foote Rd., Nevada City, CA.

Gardner, Howard. *Frames of Mind, The Theory of Multiple Intelligences*. N.Y.: Basic Books, 3rd edition, 2011.

Goodrich, Janet. *Natural Vision Improvement*. Victoria, Australia: Greenhouse Publications Pty. Ltd., 1985.

Gordon, F. Noah. *The Magical Classroom, Creating Effective, Brain-Friendly Environments for Learning*. Tucson: Zephyr Press, 1995.

Hannaford, Carla. *Education in Motion* (DVD). *heartconnnect44@aol.com*.

Hannaford, Carla: *Playing In the Unified Field, Raising and Becoming Conscious, Creative Human Beings*. Salt Lake City: Great River Books, 2010.

Hannaford, Carla. *Smart Moves, Why Learning Is Not All In Your Head*. Salt Lake City: Great River Books, 2nd ed., 2005.

Kephart, Newell C. *Movement Patterns and Motor Education*. Columbus, OH: Charles C. Merrill, 1969.

Kephart, Newell C. *The Slower Learner In the Classroom*. Columbus, OH: Charles C. Merrill, 1960.

Majoy, Peter. *Riding the Crocodile, Flying the Peach Pit*. Tucson: Zephyr Press, 1996.

Margulies, Nancy. ***Mapping Inner Space, Learning and Teaching Mind Mapping***. Tucson: Zephyr Press, 1991.

McAllen, Audrey E. ***The Extra Lesson; Exercises in Movement, Drawing and Painting for Helping Children with Difficulties with Writing, Reading and Arithmetic***. East Sussex, U.K.: Steiner Schools Fellowship Publications, 1985.

McCarthy, Bernice. ***The 4-MAT System***. Barrington, IL: Excel, Inc., 1986.

Pica, Rae. ***A Running Start, How Play, Physical Activity and Free Time Create a Successful child***. NY: Marlowe & Company, 2006.

Ratey, John and Eric Hagerman. ***SPARK, The Revolutionary New Science of Exercise and the Brain***. NY: Little Brown and Co., 2008.

Rivlin, Robert and Karen Gravelle. ***Deciphering the Senses: The Expanding World of Human Perception***. NY: Simon & Schuster, 1985.

Schwartz, Eugene. *Seeing, Hearing, Learning: The Interplay of Eye and Ear in Waldorf Education*. (Excerpts from Camp Glenbrook Conference of the Association for a Healing Education, June 14-16, 1988.) 1990. p. 12.

Thing, N.E. ***Magic Eye: A New Way of Looking at the World***. Kansas City: Andrews and McMeel, 1993.

Tomatis, Alfred A. ***The Conscious Ear, My Life of Transformation through Listening***. Barrytown, NY: Station Hill Press, 1991. pp. 208-215.

Vitale, Barbara. ***Unicorns are Real***. NY: Warner Books, 1986.

Notes

1 (page 9). MacLean, Paul. *The Triune Brain in Evolution: Role in Paleocerebral Functions.* NY: Plenum, 1990.

2 (page 16). Goddard, Sally. *A Teacher's Window into the Child's Mind . . . and Papers from the Institute for Neuro-Physiological Psychology.* Eugene, OR: Fernwood Press, 1996.

3 (page 17). Rivlin, Robert and Karen Gravelle. *Deciphering the Senses: The Expanding World of Human Perception*. NY: Simon & Schuster, 1985, p. 11. Carpenter, Siri. *Body of Thought. **Scientific American Mind**.* January/February 2011, pp. 38-45.

4 (page 17). Barsalou. Lawrence. *Grounded Cognition. **Annual Review of Psychology**.* 59: pp. 617-645, 2008.

5 (page 19). Gazzaniga, Michael S. *Human: The Science Behind What Makes Us Unique*. NY: Harper Collins, 2008.

6 (page 22). Doidge, Norman. *The Brain That Changes Itself.* NY: Viking Penguin, 2007.

7 (page 22). Sylwester, Robert. *The Role Of Wisdom In Intelligence: The Reward For An Intellectually Stimulating Life. **Brain Connection**.* www.brainconnection.com/sylwester/ March 2005.

8 (page 23). MacNeilage, Peter F., Lesley J. Rogers, Giorgio Vallortigora. *Evolutionary Origins of Your Right and Left Brain. **Scientific American**,* June 14, 2009.

9 (page 26). Bossuat, Judy Weigert. *Eye Dominance and String Playing: Does It Matter? **American String Teacher**,* February 2005, pp. 56-59.

10 (page 32). Corbailis, Michael C. *From Mouth to Hand: Gesture, Speech, and the Evolution of Right-Handedness. **Behavior and Brain Sciences**,* 26(2): pp.199-250, April 2003.

11 (page 32). *Famous Left-Handers.* www.indiana.edu/~primate/left.html

12 *(page 32).* Linke, Detief B. and Sabine Kersebaum. *Left Out.* **Scientific American Mind**, 16(4): pp. 79-63. 2005.

13 *(page 36).* Goldberg, Elkhonon. **The Wisdom Paradox, How Your Mind Can Grow Stronger as Your Brain Grows Older.** NY: Gotham Books, 2005.

14 *(page 52).* Keuroglilian, A.S. & E. J. Knudsen. *Adaptive Auditory Plasticity In Developing And Adults Animals.* **Progress in Neurobiology**, 82: pp. 109-121. 2007

15 *(page 52).* Buonomano, D.V. and M.M. Merzenich. *Cortical Plasticity: From Synapses to Maps.* **Annual Review of Neuroscience**, 21: pp. 148-186. 1998.

16 *(page 52).* Karmarkar, U.R. and Y. Dan. *Experience-dependent plasticity in adult visual cortex.* **Neuron,** 52; pp. 577-585. 2006.

17 *(page 52).* Leuthardt, Eric. **Stroke Rehabilitation.** St. Louis, MO: Center for Innovation in Neuroscience and Technology, Washington University School of Medicine, 2007.

18 *(page 52).* Doidge, Norman. **The Brain That Changes Itself.** NY: Viking Penguin, 2007.

19 *(page 126).* Vaynman, S. and F. Gomez-Pinilla. *License to Run: Exercise Impacts Functional Plasticity in the Intact and Injured Central Nervous System by Using Neurotrophins.* **Neurorehabilitation and Neural Repair**, 19(4): pp. 283-295. Dec. 2005.

20 *(page 127).* Dorothy G. Singer, Roberta Michnich-Golinkoff and Kathy Hirsh-Posek (editors). **Play = Learning: How Play Motivates and Enhances Children's Cognitive and Social-Emotional Growth.** NY: Oxford University Press. 2006

21 *(page 128).* Pellis, Sergio M., and Vivian C. Pellis. *Rough-and-Tumble Play and the Development of the Social Brain.* **Current Directions in Psychological Science.** 16(2): pp. 95-98, April 2007.

22 *(page 128).* Glauslusz, Josie. *Living In A Dream World.* **Scientific American Mind**, March/April 2011, pp. 24-31.

23 *(page 128).* Nolen-Hoeksena, Susan, et al. *Rethinking Rumination.* **Perspectives on Psychological Science.** 3(5): pp. 400-424. 2008.

24 (page 130). Ramscar, Michael, et al. The *Effects of Feature-Label-Order and Their Implications for Symbolic Learning.* **Cognitive Science**. 34(6), pp. 909-957. Aug. 2010.

25 (page 133). Fischer, Burkhart. A Sensory Fix for Problems in School. **Scientific American Mind**. March/April 2010, pp. 32-37.

26 (page 133). Fischer, Burkhart. **Looking for Learning: Auditory, Visual and Optomotor Processing in Children with Learning Problems.** Hauppauge, NY: Nova Science Publisher. 2006.

27 (page 150). Mattson, A., et. al. *40 Hertz EEG Activity in Learning Disabled and Normal Children.* Poster presentation, International Neuropsychological Society, Vancouver, B.C. February, 1989.

28 (page 151). Brewer, Chris & Don Campbell. **Rhythms of Learning, Creative Tools for Developing Lifelong Skills.** Tucson: Zephyr Press, 1991.

29 (page 158). Wheatley, Grayson H. *The Right Hemisphere's Role in Problems Solving.* **Arithmetic Teacher**. 11: pp. 36-39, 1977.

30 (page 159). Samples, Bob. *Educating for Both Sides of the Human Mind.* **The Science Teacher**, January 1975, pp. 21-23.

31 (page 159). Epstein, Herman T. *Growth Spurts During Brain Development: Implications for Educational Policy and Practice.* J. Chall & A.F. Mirsky (eds.), **Education and the Brain**. Chicago: University of Chicago Press, 1979, pp. 343-370.

32 (page 165). Goodheart, George. **Applied Kinesiology, Workshop Procedure Manual.** (Privately published.) Detroit, 1987.

33 (page 165). Walther, David S. **Applied Kinesiology**. Pueblo, Colorado: Synopsis Systems, 1988.

34 (page 165). Kendall, H., Kendall, F., Wadsworth G. **Muscle Testing and Function**. Baltimore: Williams & Wilkins, 1971.

35 (page 165) Leisman, Gerald, Shambaugh and Avery Ferentz. *Somatosensory evoked potential changes during muscle testing.* **Internal J. Neuroscience,** 45: pp. 143-151, 1989.

[36] *(page 165)* Leisman, Gerald; Zenhausern, Robert, et. al. *Electromyographic effects of fatigue and task repetition on the validity of estimates of strong and weak muscles in applied kinesiological muscle-testing procedures.* **Perceptual and Motor Skills Journal**, 80: pp. 963-977, 1995.

[37] *(page 165).* Schaafsma A., Ohen, E., von Willigen, J.D. *A Muscle spindle model for primary afferent firing based on a simulation of intrafusal mechanical events.* **J. Neurophysiology** 65: p. 1297, 1991.

[38] *(page 165).* Hasan, Z. and Houk, J. *Analysis of response properties of deefferented mammalian spindle receptors based on frequency of response.* **J. Neurophysiol.** 38: pp. 663-672, 1975. Hasan, Z. and Houk, J. *Transition in sensitivity of spindle receptors that occurs when muscle is stretched more than a fraction of a millimeter.* **J. Neurophysiol.** 38: pp. 673-389, 1975.

[39] *(page 165).* Monti, Daniel A., Kunkel, Elisabeth, et. al. *Muscle test comparisons of congruent and incongruent self-referential statements.* **Perceptual and Motor Skills Journal**, 88: pp. 1019-1028, 1999.

[40] *(page 167).* Perot, C., Meldener R., and F. Goubel. *Objective measurement of proprioceptive technique consequences on muscular maximal voluntary contraction during manual muscle testing.* **Agressologie.** Université de technologie, Compiegne, 32 (10 Spec. No.): pp. 471-474, 1991.

Index

C

D

E

V

W

Y

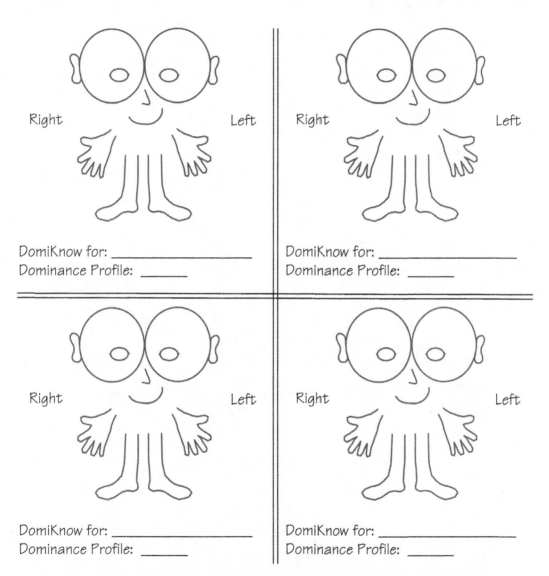

Right   Left   Right   Left

DomiKnow for: _____   DomiKnow for: _____
Dominance Profile: _____   Dominance Profile: _____

Right   Left   Right   Left

DomiKnow for: _____   DomiKnow for: _____
Dominance Profile: _____   Dominance Profile: _____

Carla Hannaford, Ph.D. is a biologist and educator with more than fifty years of teaching experience, including twenty years teaching biology at the university level and four years as a counselor for elementary and intermediate school children with learning difficulties.

She is an internationally recognized educational consultant, having presented more than six hundred lectures and workshops in thirty-five countries over the past two decades. She was selected as a guest educator with the AHP-Soviet Project in 1988, has been recognized by Who's Who in American Education, and has received awards from the University of Hawaii and the American Association for the Advancement of Science for outstanding teaching in science. She has advised ministries and departments of education in the United States, Russia, South Africa, Singapore, and Scotland.

Her most recent book is **_Playing in the Unified Field, Raising & Becoming Conscious, Creative Human Beings_** (Great River Books, 2010), a far-reaching exploration of the intersection of the latest developments in the fields of science, consciousness and education, Her first book, **_Smart Moves; Why Learning Is Not All In Your Head_**, first published in 1995 and updated in 2005 (Great River Books), has been translated into a dozen languages. She is also the author of **_Awakening The Child Heart, Handbook for Global Parenting_**, (Jamilla Nur Publishing, 2002) She authored and co-produced the video **_Education in Motion_**, and co-presented her work with Candace Pert and Susan Kovalik on the video **_Emotions: Gateway to Learning_**. She has contributed hundreds of articles to educational and science journals and magazines and been featured in scores of radio and TV interviews in the U.S. and abroad.

She lives with her musician husband Ahti Mohala in Montana.